Renaissance monarchies

CAMBRIDGE PERSPECTIVES IN HISTORY

Series editors: **Richard Brown and David Smith**

Other theme texts in the series include:

The Tudor monarchies, 1461–1603   John McGurk   0 521 59665 3
Authority and disorder in Tudor times, 1461–1603   Paul Thomas   0 521 62664 1
Papists, Protestants and Puritans, 1559–1714   Diana Newton   0 521 59845 1
British imperialism, 1750–1970   Simon C. Smith   0 521 59930 X
Democracy and the role of the state, 1830–1945   Michael Willis   0 521 59994 6
A disunited kingdom, 1800–1945   Christine Kinealy   0 521 59844 3
Chartism   Richard Brown   0 521 58617 8

Nationalism in Europe, 1789–1945   Timothy Baycroft   0 521 59871 0
Revolutions, 1789–1917   Allan Todd   0 521 58600 3
The origins of the First and Second World Wars   Frank McDonough   0 521 56861 7
Fascism   Richard Thurlow   0 521 59872 9
Nazi Germany   Frank McDonough   0 521 59502 9
The Holocaust   Peter Neville   0 521 59501 0

Renaissance monarchies, 1469–1558

Catherine Mulgan

CAMBRIDGE
UNIVERSITY PRESS

PUBLISHED BY THE PRESS SYNDICATE OF THE UNIVERSITY OF CAMBRIDGE
The Pitt Building, Trumpington Street, Cambridge CB2 1RP, United Kingdom

CAMBRIDGE UNIVERSITY PRESS
The Edinburgh Building, Cambridge CB2 2RU, United Kingdom
40 West 20th Street, New York, NY 10011–4211, USA
10 Stamford Road, Oakleigh, Melbourne 3166, Australia

First published 1998

Printed in the United Kingdom at the University Press, Cambridge

Typeset in Tiepolo and Formata

A catalogue record for this book is available from the British Library

ISBN 0 521 59870 2 paperback

Text design by Newton Harris Design Partnership

Map illustrations by Kathy Baxendale

Acknowledgements
Cover, British Library, London/Bridgeman Art Library, London/New York (Add
33733f.9); 5, Prado, Madrid/Index/Bridgeman Art Library, London/New York;
29, Louvre, Paris, AKG, London; 46, AKG, London; 61, Alte Pinakothek,
Munich/Giraudon/Bridgeman Art Library, London/New York; 68, Louvre, Paris,
France/Bridgeman Art Library, London/New York; 101, Bridgeman Art Library,
London/New York

The cover illustration shows the raising of the siege of Vienna, 1529, illuminated
by Giulio Clovio, in *The triumphs of the emperor Charles V*, Rome, c. 1556.

Contents

Contents

Introduction

The 'new monarchy' is a term used by many historians to describe the kings and queens who took a decisive step on the road from feudal to absolute rule during the period covered by this book. As they lived at the time when the Italian Renaissance was making its impact on the rest of Europe, it is also justifiable to call them 'Renaissance monarchs'. They come between medieval rulers, with their limited power and resources, and the far mightier autocrats of the seventeenth and eighteenth centuries (of whom Louis XIV is the most famous).

These monarchs had to face challenges not encountered by their predecessors. Two of the most obvious are the fall in the value of money (inflation) and the huge increase in the size and equipment of fighting forces. Most of these rulers also had to respond to the Protestant Reformation, which threatened the political as well as the religious unity of their countries.

Rising costs stimulated each government to make its financial machinery more effective, and to seek new sources of income. Inevitably, tightening up one branch of administration led to the strengthening of other aspects of government. In the search for closer control over their resources, these rulers took a more rigorous hold over their nobility, their churchmen, their judicial systems and their representative bodies (*Parlements, Estates, Cortes* and town councils). When this provoked protest, or even revolt, opponents were dealt with severely.

Every one of the monarchs in this book was a devout Catholic; in Spain the challenge to this faith came from the Muslims and Jews and had existed for centuries. In France and Germany, the rising tide of Protestantism posed the problem and caused civil war in both countries (although this did not come to France till after Francis I's death).

These rulers each responded in his or her own way to the general challenges, as well as to those particular to their individual kingdoms. Yet there are many features common to their reigns (which they share with Henry VII and VIII of England). It is for this reason that terms such as 'new monarchy' and 'Renaissance monarchies' can be useful.

Ferdinand and Isabella inherited kingdoms that were weak and divided by civil wars and the presence of over-powerful nobles. They chose to use their military power to conquer the last Muslim area in Spain. Once that task was complete, they had at their disposal the energy and resources needed for expansion across the Atlantic and into southern Italy.

Their grandson Charles, as king of Spain, inherited their combined kingdoms, as well as an expanding overseas empire which brought new problems but also fabulous riches. Yet the greater part of Charles's time and energy was devoted to his other responsibility, the Holy Roman Empire. Here he ruled a mass of semi-independent states that resented any attempt to bring them under central control. When Luther's message spread rapidly through these lands, it was taken up as a German national cause; Charles lacked the resources and the ruthlessness to suppress it until it had taken a firm hold. In the end, the problems of his huge territories broke him, both physically and mentally, and he abdicated.

The French king, Francis I, inherited a country with fewer obvious problems, and great resources. Yet he chose to devote much of his reign to campaigns to conquer lands in Italy, with no lasting success. Obsessed by the threat of Charles V (who ruled lands encircling France on all sides), he wasted the benefits of his financial reforms by spending the money raised on yet further wars. But the king also spent money with lasting results on magnificent royal palaces and on patronage of the arts.

The foreign policies of these three countries, France, Spain and the Holy Roman Empire, consist of a constantly changing pattern of alliances as England, the popes and the rulers of other Italian states became involved in the long-drawn-out struggle between them. This had started with the French invasion of Italy in 1494, and did not end until the Treaty of Cateau-Cambrésis in 1559.

The term 'Renaissance monarchies' conjures up an image of rulers in rich clothing, portrayed in postures of power. Francis I and Charles V were both painted by Titian in this mode, while Henry VIII was similarly served by Holbein. Ferdinand and Isabella, like Henry VII, belonged to the previous generation who had not realised the possibilities of art as a tool of propaganda, and were content to be painted in a simpler style.

These rulers are interesting individuals in their own right, and deserve to be remembered for notable achievements, as well as for the failures that they left for their successors to face. Each devoted much time and energy to the business of ruling, and acted in what he or she saw as the best interests of their country at that time.

1 Ferdinand and Isabella: domestic policy

The stone figures of Ferdinand and Isabella lie side-by-side in Granada Cathedral on a splendid monument inscribed 'The Destroyers of Islam and Heresy'. Not long before her death, Isabella wrote a short assessment of her achievements and failures as an addition to her will. It starts with the conquest of Granada and the success of the Inquisition in rooting out heresy, the two victories commemorated on the tomb. But it continues with her shame that the hopes of restoring the crown's resources had not been fully realised; at her death, she believed that taxation was still unjust and that the nobility kept far too much of the country's wealth.

Yet, in Spain, there remains a tradition that the 'Catholic monarchs', as Ferdinand and Isabella were always known, achieved a huge restoration of royal authority and laid the foundations for eventual Spanish unity. Until recently, they were also regarded by historians as one of the 'new monarchies' of late fifteenth-century Europe, along with the kings of England and France, who successfully imposed greater royal power at a similar time. The most recent opinion, however, is that the strength of the crown in Spain was restored rather than extended at this stage.

The condition of Aragon and Castile

To assess the reality of Ferdinand and Isabella's achievement, the country and the problems they inherited must first be considered.

Spain was unlike any other west European state in her long confrontation with Islam. It had taken many centuries to drive back the Muslim conquerors, a process known as *Reconquista* (Reconquest). During this time, new kingdoms were created as new areas returned to Christian control. By the time of Ferdinand and Isabella's accession, the country consisted of three independent kingdoms: Castile (which included, for example, León), Aragon (which included Catalonia and Valencia) and Portugal. In the south-east lay the small Muslim kingdom of Granada.

Another point of difference from the rest of Europe was the presence of large Muslim and Jewish populations among the Christians. Many had converted, at least superficially, and reached high office and great wealth. When times grew hard, these people began to arouse resentment and became convenient scapegoats for the country's troubles. Their contribution to the life of the whole community was undervalued and, eventually, they were expelled. This deprived Spain of their skills as well as their capital.

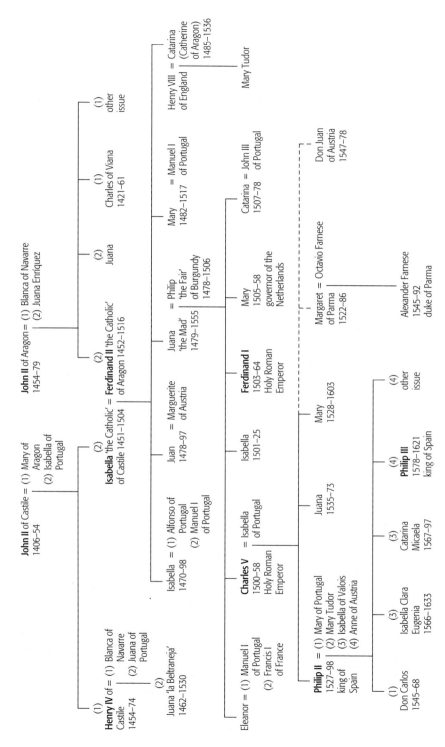

The Spanish royal house in the fifteenth and sixteenth centuries.

At the same time, the presence of Granada was a constant reminder that *Reconquista* had not been completed and that Christianity was still a religion under threat. This helps to explain the enormous power of the Roman Catholic church in Spain. It was seen as the great bulwark of the nation, and was easily able to rally resources to its defence. Jealous of papal interference, it worked hand-in-hand with the monarchy, so that religious needs dominated crown policy.

No one yet used the word 'Spain' in the modern sense; people considered themselves to be, for example, Aragonese, Catalan or Castilian. Not since the time of Roman *Hispania* had the country been united, and only a handful of humanist scholars dreamt of restoring it. When Ferdinand of Aragon married Isabella of Castile in 1469, few foresaw that this would eventually lead to the

The Virgin of the Catholic kings. A fifteenth-century painting of the Virgin Mary, flanked by Ferdinand and Isabella (Flemish/Hispanic, 1490, by Spanish School).

unified kingdom of Spain. Many such marriages between rulers of separate states have had no such permanent effect.

Aragon

Aragon had completed its *Reconquista* from Islam long ago. It had since developed a flourishing city life, particularly in its ports such as Barcelona, and had good trade links with the Mediterranean. The coastal plain of Valencia provided rich soil for agriculture. The power of Aragon's kings was limited by a complex series of institutions and legal rights, and each region had its own powerful *Cortes* (parliament). New laws had to be approved by the *Cortes* in all three regions, and there were strict rules for the regular summoning of the *Cortes* and who should attend. Another brake on royal power was the official known as the *Justiciar* whose task was to see that officials did not infringe the law or damage individual citizens by the use of arbitrary methods.

During John II's reign from 1458 to 1479, in spite of a long tradition of rights and responsibilities held in balance, order had broken down in Aragon. In 1479, he left his son, Ferdinand, a country in political chaos and economic decline. Badly hit by the Black Death, Catalonia was losing its trade links to Genoese and other competitors. In the towns, the richer and poorer inhabitants fought to control the diminishing sources of wealth. In the countryside, landlords and tenants were at odds because of a shortage of land that could be cultivated.

Castile

Castile, on the other hand, was enjoying an economic upsurge. Although it consisted largely of arid, mountainous country, this was well-suited to sheep rearing, which required little capital and labour compared to crop cultivation. The government encouraged sheep farmers and wool exports because they were easy to control, and simple to tax. An institution called the *Mesta* controlled the huge sheep migrations between summer and winter pastures, and prevented crop cultivation in all the areas needed for these journeys. With the wool trade booming, the government did not worry that Castile had to import corn whenever there was a bad harvest. Nor were they concerned that the peasants were sinking into ever greater poverty, for very few owned their land, unlike in Aragon. The great noble families, who owned the bulk of the land, were unconcerned as long as they enjoyed the great wealth and the political power which had been theirs for so long.

Few Castilians were town-dwellers, and the small middle class usually found itself excluded from running urban affairs by the powerful local nobles. Everything in Castile seemed to work in favour of the aristocrats. This was the class that had reaped the benefits of *Reconquista* in the form of huge grants of land, exemption from taxation and a great measure of control over their tenants. Weak kings had done little to curb their powers and privileges, which included tax exemption and the right to trial in special courts. At the same time, the Castilian *Cortes* was far weaker than that of Aragon, so the way was open for a determined monarch further to increase the power of the crown. No one had the

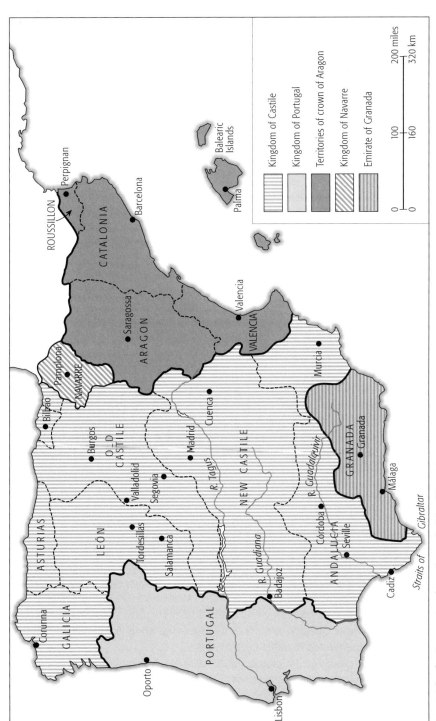

Map 1. The Iberian peninsula at the end of the fifteenth century.

right to be summoned to Castile's *Cortes*. Monarchs were under no obligation to summon it, and the monarch could pass laws without its approval. Unlike the Aragonese *Cortes*, the Castilian *Cortes* lacked the power to make redress of grievances a condition of granting more money.

Aragon and Castile each kept its own coinage and its own language, and valued its separate identity. In Castile, the fact that *Reconquista* was not over meant that this still put its stamp on the whole of Castilian life. For this reason, the values of the soldier, honour and courage rather than hard work and security, were those most widely admired. The typical soldier was the *hidalgo*, or lesser noble, and his snobbishness as well as his macho image permeated Castilian society. Aspirants to this privileged status would go to extraordinary lengths to produce family trees proving that a distant ancestor had noble blood.

Ferdinand and Isabella's marriage

In 1469, Ferdinand was seventeen, and heir to his father John II, king of Aragon. Threatened by rebellion in Catalonia, and with the French king keen to extend his frontiers at Aragon's expense, John hoped that a marriage alliance might bring him some Castilian help in his troubles. Isabella of Castile's position was even more difficult. Her half-brother, Henry, king of Castile, recognised Isabella as his heir, but a powerful faction supported Henry's daughter, Juana, whose legitimacy was doubtful. Isabella also had two other suitors, a French prince and the king of Portugal, who was an elderly widower, favoured by her brother. Hardly surprisingly, the eighteen-year-old Isabella preferred Ferdinand, and was willing to endure danger and difficulty to marry him. She was, however, determined to keep control of Castile in her own hands once she was queen; the pair would live in Castile, which was by far the larger of the two kingdoms. Ferdinand agreed to take second place in its government, although it was later agreed that he would take responsibility for foreign policy for both countries. There was to be no merger between Aragon and Castile; each would continue to be run as a separate unit. Since the two were so different in language, customs, political structure and economy, no other plan was even considered.

But, when Ferdinand and Isabella married in 1469, neither had yet succeeded to their respective kingdoms. Isabella was proclaimed queen in 1474, when her brother Henry IV died, but she had to fight her half-sister, Juana, backed by Alfonso of Portugal and nobles who feared that Ferdinand's support would help to increase the strength of the crown. The civil war was not over till 1479, when Juana was defeated and put away in a convent. Earlier that year, Ferdinand's father had died and he had succeeded him as king of Aragon, where, in the 1460s, there had also been civil war.

Joint rule

From such an uncertain start, Ferdinand and Isabella forged one of the most effective partnerships in royal history. Although very different in character, they shared the same objectives and were warmly attached to each other. Isabella was deeply pious, stoical in adversity (she suffered many close family deaths) and morally upright, while Ferdinand's word could not be trusted and he was often unfaithful to her. They both signed royal decrees and were always spoken of in one breath as 'Ferdinand and Isabella' or the 'Catholic Monarchs', the title that had been granted them by Pope Alexander VI. They viewed kingship as a 'hands-on' occupation, endlessly travelling round their territories to supervise administration and justice. As there was no fixed capital, the court and its entourage of officials was constantly on the move.

Isabella came to allow Ferdinand a far greater share in the government of Castile than she had originally envisaged, while he left Aragon in the care of viceroys. In fact, Castile was increasingly the senior partner; in addition to its far bigger population (7 million compared to Aragon's 1 million), the country began to experience a sharp upsurge of national confidence. This was fuelled by a surplus of energy that remained once *Reconquista* was complete in 1492 (see page 17), just at the time when Aragon was in decline.

The restoration of order

The two kingdoms were both in desperate need of firm and just government by the time the new rulers finally gained control. Ordinary citizens longed for order and security after years of civil war, and gladly supported the two monarchs in their campaign to provide protection against the arrogance and greed of the magnates. Ferdinand and Isabella saw the restoration of the crown's rights and authority going hand-in-hand with care for the rights of the poor. To achieve these aims, they passed hundreds of edicts and built up existing organs of government to restore justice and strengthen government authority. Political power was largely taken away from the great nobles and given to royal officials appointed from the lesser gentry and middle class, especially lawyers.

Aragon

Before turning his attention to Castile, however, Ferdinand had to bring order to Aragon. Here his policy was different from that undertaken in the larger kingdom; existing rights and institutions were confirmed and made more effective, not over-ruled to bring greater crown control. There was no attempt to bring the two kingdoms into line with a view to an eventual merger. Ferdinand helped build up a class of peasant proprietors by abolishing feudal dues and giving effective possession of their land to the better-off peasants. In the towns, he put all public posts up for distribution by lot, to break the hold of self-perpetuating cliques. The Catalan *Corts* (the Catalan form of *Cortes*) had, for centuries, enjoyed far greater freedom to oppose royal demands than, for example, had the *Cortes* in Castile. It now re-asserted the entire system of political checks on royal power laid down in its constitution, and Ferdinand accepted this. In 1494, the Council of Aragon was created to supervise the kingdom; like all the royal councils, it was staffed by a core of lawyer-officials and based in Castile.

Castile

Meanwhile, in Castile, a *Cortes* summoned to Madrigal in 1476 had begun the process of restoring royal authority. Bandits had been free to terrorise both town and country during the civil war; to stop this, Ferdinand and Isabella revived the medieval town brotherhood of the Santa Hermandad and turned it into a local police force. It was also told to provide tribunals of magistrates to try the culprits, and the two arms of the brotherhood rooted out banditry between them.

Another *Cortes*, held at Toledo in 1480, passed an Act of Resumption. This took back into crown hands the revenues that the magnates had illegally seized during the years of weak royal control. It also laid down the composition of the Royal Council of Castile as the central governing body for the country. The Royal Council of Castile acted as a supreme court of justice, as well as supervising both central and local government. It was vital to keep this body out of the grip of the great aristocrats, so its membership was closely controlled. The full members included a churchman and a handful of officials, to be joined each Friday by the king and queen. Holders of the traditional top positions could still attend, but could not vote; their jobs became purely ceremonial.

In this way, political power was taken away from the great families and given instead to the lesser gentry and to well-educated men from the towns, including Jewish converts to Christianity, the *conversos*. Increasingly, a university education, preferably in law, was the route to a good government position.

One important post, newly extended, was that of a *corregidor*. These men were appointed by the government to all the main towns to supervise justice and administration and were used as a means of tightening royal control over the towns of Castile. At the same time, rules were laid down to promote greater efficiency; for example, town halls had to be built and detailed administrative records kept. Ferdinand and Isabella took a close personal interest in all major appointments, showing good judgement in their selections. They also played a role in the country's judicial system. Every Friday they heard individual cases, and also set up a system of appeal courts for defendants dissatisfied with the justice they had received locally.

It was vital to increase crown income alongside crown authority. Ferdinand and Isabella managed to increase the royal revenue from 900,000 *reales* in 1474, to 26,000,000 in 1504. This was not achieved by tax increases, except in the last four of these years, but largely by making the existing machinery more effective, and through the growth in national wealth. The most dramatic rise was in the yield of the *alcabala*, the 10 per cent sales tax (roughly equivalent to VAT). The recovery of the revenues seized by the nobility also helped, so did the acquisition of the wealth of the three Religious and Military Orders of medieval Castile. When death created vacancies, Ferdinand was able to become the Grand Master of the Three Orders and to acquire for the crown their huge estates and revenues and their vast powers of patronage. A Royal Council of Military Orders was created to run them. Eventually, in 1523, a papal bull incorporated all three into the crown.

The church

Extending royal authority

The church was another hugely wealthy and powerful body that Ferdinand and Isabella believed should be brought more firmly under royal authority. Like the nobility, the clergy were exempt from taxation. Bishops and cathedral chapters owned vast estates which lay outside crown control. Isabella was an intensely devout woman, which led her to take a close interest in the affairs of the church, and fired her ambition to root out corruption and raise the moral and educational standards of the clergy. She supported the foundation of a theological college at Valladolid, and the new university at Alcalá, and also the reform of the orders of monks and friars undertaken by Cardinal Cisneros, archbishop of Toledo (also known as Ximenes).

An Ecclesiastical Council, called in 1478, was asked to support Ferdinand and Isabella in their campaign to wrest control of church appointments from the pope. Later, they demanded and received the right to make all the church appointments in the newly acquired region of Granada, and eventually in the new lands across the Atlantic. They also won control over church revenues, including a third of all the tithes in Castile, and the special tax to finance war against the Muslims, the *cruzada*, which continued to be collected long after Granada had fallen.

At a time when the Roman Catholic church elsewhere in Europe was under attack, the church in Spain was putting its own house in order and emerging with fresh vigour. However, this new energy was also channelled into a growing intolerance of non-Christians and recent converts to Christianity. Ferdinand was himself partly Jewish, and began his reign by employing many *conversos*, but their growing wealth and influence started to cause resentment. They were also accused of secretly practising their old religion and mixing with unconverted Jews.

The establishment of the Inquisition

Ferdinand and Isabella were persuaded to apply to Rome in 1478 for permission to establish the Inquisition in Castile. (A half-hearted version had existed in Aragon since the thirteenth century to deal with Jewish converts.) Its task was to examine new Christians accused of backsliding and, when necessary, to punish them. The objective was complete purity of faith, since religious unity was thought to be the essential basis of national unity. Nine years later, the Inquisition in its new form was installed in Aragon as well. It was the only institution (apart from the crown itself) that was common to both kingdoms. Although Ferdinand lacked Isabella's deep piety and high morality, he was a fervent supporter of the church, and saw that the Inquisition could be an instrument of political, as well as religious, control, through its network of informers. From 1483, the Inquisition was under the control of a royal council.

By 1492, Ferdinand and Isabella felt that the conquest of Granada (see page 17) had solved the question of the Muslims; it was now time to turn their attention to the Jews. An edict threatened all those who failed to convert to Christianity within four months with expulsion. Between 120,000 and 150,000 Jews left the country, taking their capital with them as well as their skills. They left gaps in the country's commercial life that foreigners were quick to fill. The difference was that the newcomers exploited Spain's wealth, while the Jews had enriched it, so the whole economy was weakened.

The economy

Strengthening the economy within Spain

At the same time, Ferdinand and Isabella were keen to improve the country's economy, but their policies were often counter-productive. The wool trade was one of those which suffered from the departure of the Jewish merchants. Sheep farmers contributed to royal revenues through a special tax; but the protection they received in return was given at the expense of other forms of agriculture. In Castile, 97 per cent of the land was owned by under 3 per cent of the population; the great families leased their land to sheep rearers and grew even richer on the profits.

The fairs at Medina del Campo were reorganised, and a combined guild-cum-mercantile court was established at Burgos. This gave the city a complete monopoly over the entire wool trade. From there, the wool was taken to Bilbao and shipped to Antwerp, and exports continued to expand under this central control. Yet, in other trades and industries, such as silk, the guilds and the crown interference were a brake on innovation and expansion. Roads were improved, but customs barriers between the various provinces hampered trade. Nothing was done to integrate the economies of Castile and Aragon, based on the Atlantic and the Mediterranean respectively. In fact, Aragonese traders were deliberately excluded from the new market in the Americas.

Trade with the Americas

Perhaps the greatest of the royal controls on the economy was the monopoly of trade with the Americas given to Seville (see page 34). In 1503, the House of Trade was set up on the bank of the Guadalquivir River, which brought ocean-going ships up to Seville. It was given total control of all trade with the new lands across the Atlantic; all goods destined for shipment to the Americas, and all the raw materials and precious metals sent eastwards from the Americas to Europe, passed through Seville. One fifth of all the bullion shipments went straight to the crown and became, in later years, a vast source of income. Almost at once, the value of the cargoes made it practical to organise the transatlantic shipping into convoys with armed escorts. The city of Seville grew dramatically, and newcomers poured in from all over Castile to share in the boom; but this was only in its very early stages in the time of the Catholic kings.

Isabella's death in 1504

Isabella died in 1504, which meant that Ferdinand was no longer king of Castile. The rightful ruler was Ferdinand and Isabella's second daughter, Juana. Isabella, their eldest daughter, had died after being briefly married to the king of Portugal. Juana was married to Philip of Burgundy, but known to be mentally unstable, and, therefore, excluded from a share in running the country. Philip was impatient to get his hands on his wife's inheritance, and Castilian nobles, who had lost out under Ferdinand and Isabella's policies, were keen to curry favour with the coming ruler. Some of them even travelled to Brussels to make their faces known at the Burgundian court before Philip left it.

Although Philip was a weak character, he resented any hint that his authority in Castile might be limited. In the event, when he and Juana finally arrived at Corunna, in Castile, in 1506, the bulk of the nobility expressed its support for him. Ferdinand was forced to hand over the government of Castile and retire to Aragon. But Philip died almost at once, and his wife collapsed into total madness (she kept her husband's corpse and insisted it accompanied her wherever she went). A Regency Council was set up, with Cardinal Cisneros as president, to run Castile on behalf of six-year-old Charles, Philip and Juana's son. However, disorder spread so quickly that Ferdinand was invited back in 1510 as administrator of Castile. The real day-to-day rule was still in the hands of Cisneros, and Ferdinand was free to devote his last years to foreign policy.

Ferdinand and Isabella's legacy

What had been achieved? Ferdinand and Isabella had taken away some of the grandees' political influence, but the great families still had huge economic and social power. Grants of newly conquered lands in Granada had further increased their strength; on their own estates they were still immensely strong throughout the kingdoms. The increasing poverty of the landless peasants of Castile was ignored as the wool trade continued to flourish. The religious unity of the country had been brought nearer at terrible cost to its Muslim and Jewish inhabitants. Yet in spite of the seeds of future trouble that were sown in these years, there is justification for looking back on the reign of Ferdinand and Isabella as a 'golden age'. The church had been strengthened, Granada won, royal authority and order restored. It was also a time of huge intellectual and artistic excitement. Isabella's reputation as a patron attracted European humanist scholars to Castile. She and Ferdinand were great builders of palaces as well as hospitals and universities. Christian culture was enriched by its contact with Muslim and Jewish ideas and styles, one result being a uniquely Spanish architectural style. Castilian became the dominant language as Castile became the dominant partner; to Castilians, Castile was Spain. The Union of Crowns had helped pave the way for the eventual emergence of one country from two.

Document case studies

Isabella's character

1.1 Isabella's sense of purpose

Isabella speaking to a contemporary in 1474

I have come to this land and I certainly do not intend to leave it to flee danger nor shirk work, nor will I give such glory to my enemies nor such pain to my subjects.

Source: P. K. Liss, *Isabel the queen*, New York, 1992

1.2 A prayer composed by Isabella

Quoted by Hernando del Pulgar, who was secretary and chronicler to Ferdinand, in his Crónica de los reyes Católicos

You, Lord, who know the secret of every heart, you know of me that not by unjust means, not with cunning, nor tyranny, but believing truly that these kingdoms of the King my father by right belong to me, I have sought to have them so that what the kings my forebears won with so much bloodshed may not pass to a foreign lineage. And you, Lord, in whose hands is the right of kingdoms, through the dictates of your Providence, you have put me in this royal state in which I am today. I implore humbly, My Lord, that you hear now the prayer of your servant, and show the truth, and manifest your will with your marvellous works. If I do not have justice, may there be no room for me to sin through ignorance, and if I do have justice, may you give me intelligence and strength so that, with the help of your arm, I can pursue and achieve my charge, and bring peace in these kingdoms, which have suffered so many evils and such destruction.

Source: P. K. Liss, *Isabel the queen*, New York, 1992

1.3 Isabella's speech during the civil war, 1475

An anonymous chronicler's verbatim account

I find myself in my palace, with angry heart and closed teeth and clenched fists, as if, seeking revenge, I am fighting with myself . . . Of my fury, being a woman, and of your patience, being men, I marvel . . . And what greater honour, greater benefit, what greater service to God, could there be than joining battle? . . . If you say to me that women, since they do not face such dangers, ought not to speak of them . . . to this I say that I do not know who risks more than I do, for I risked my King and Lord, whom I love above all else in the world, and I risked so many and such noble *caballeros*, [knights] and so many men and riches that, they lost, what more would I have to venture?

Source: P. K. Liss, *Isabel the queen*, New York, 1992

1.4 Ferdinand's alleged reply to Isabella

Ferdinand to Isabella, on his return after the defeat of the Portuguese army at the Battle of Toro, 1476 (letter)

Give repose, My Lady, to the anxieties of your heart, for the time and days to come will bring you such victories, that, even if they defeat us in this one, for a thousand won you will pardon us this one lost . . . I had believed that returning in despair I would hear from your tongue words of consolation and encouragement . . . Women are always malcontent, and you especially, My Lady, since the man who would satisfy you is yet to be born.

Source: P. K. Liss, *Isabel the queen*, New York, 1992

1.5 A contemporary view of Isabella

From Hernando del Pulgar's Crónica de los reyes Católicos

It was certainly a thing most marvellous, that what many men and great lords did not manage to do in many years, a single woman did in a short time through work and governance.

Source: P. K. Liss, *Isabel the queen*, New York, 1992

Document case-study questions

1 Who are the 'enemies' referred to in 1.1, and what danger did Isabella face?

2 Identify the 'foreign lineage' in 1.2 who might inherit 'these kingdoms'.

3 What does Isabella's prayer in 1.2 reveal about her views on a ruler's relationship with God?

4 What light is thrown on the relationship between Ferdinand and Isabella by extracts 1.3, 1.4 and 1.5?

5 Is Pulgar's assessment in 1.5 a just one?

6 What aspects of Isabella's character and beliefs are shown in these documents, and how far is this a full portrait?

Ferdinand and Isabella: the Inquisition and the Jews

1.6 The work of the Inquisition in Andalucia

From Hernando del Pulgar's Crónica de los reyes Católicos

The establishment of the Inquisition, indispensable recourse to punish the depraved heresy had also augmented penury . . . It is certain that this was considered trivial in respect to eternal happiness, since true riches are the possession of true Catholics. Thus Don Fernando and Doña Isabel put before any inconvenience whatever the ripping out of the multitude of judaizers from among the Andalucian people, so that those infected by error would return to the road of eternal health by means of a true reconciliation or would perish among the flames if they remained obdurate . . . among *conversos* most women practised Jewish rites.

Source: P. K. Liss, *Isabel the queen*, New York, 1992

1.7 Ferdinand on the occasion of the extension of the Inquisition into Aragon

Ferdinand writing in 1484 (letter)

Before we decided to allow this Inquisition to act in any city . . . we had considered all the harm that might result to our royal rights and revenues. But since Our firm intention and zeal is to place the service of Our Lord God before our own . . . we wish that this should be done, and all other interests put aside.

Source: P. K. Liss, *Isabel the queen*, New York, 1992

1.8 Punishments for supposed Christians performing Jewish rites throughout Aragon

Ferdinand and Isabella in an order of 1484

. . . and all their property, of which there was a great quantity, applied to the *Cámara* [treasury] of the King and Queen . . . and the Queen commanded that they should not be distributed for any purpose except in the war against the Moors and other things that were for the exaltation of the Catholic faith.

Source: W. T. Walsh, *Isabella of Spain*, London, 1931

1.9 Contemporary Christian comment on the Jews of Castile and Aragon

Hostile words from a parish priest

All their work was to multiply and increase . . . they never wanted to take manual work, ploughing or digging . . . but only jobs in the towns, so as to sit around making money without doing much work.

Source: W. T. Walsh, *Isabella of Spain*, London, 1931

Document case-study questions

7 Explain the words 'judaizers' and '*conversos*' in 1.6.

8 In the context of 1.6, what is meant by 'true riches'?

9 What arguments for and against the action taken by Ferdinand and Isabella are shared by 1.6 and 1.7?
What doubt is cast on these justifications in 1.8?

10 What light is shed on Christian hatred of the Jews in 1.9?

11 How far do these documents show the real reasons for the establishment of the Inquisition by Ferdinand and Isabella?

2 Ferdinand and Isabella: foreign policy

The conquest of Granada

In 1474, the Muslim kingdom of Granada still survived on Castile's southern border after nearly eight hundred years: it was the last bastion of Islam on Spanish soil. It also lay across an intricate network of trade routes, and was the last obstacle to control over the political, religious and economic life of the country as a whole. Once the civil wars in Aragon and Castile were over, and the initial moves to restore order and royal authority had begun to take effect, Ferdinand and Isabella were determined to conquer it.

Granada's continuing independence was always a potential threat to Spanish security as it provided a possible base for an invader. It was, however, primarily as a crusade against Islam that the campaign stirred the imagination and aroused the ardour of Castile's Christians (and to a lesser extent, those of Aragon as well). Ferdinand and Isabella realised its worth as a truly nation-wide cause. It could unite their divided subjects, harness the energy of restless young men and, as a bonus, give a great boost to Spanish prestige. Capturing Muslim territory had always held out the promise of booty and new estates for the victors, as well as military glory.

Reconquista was a very long-established activity, that had only come to a halt during Castile and Aragon's civil wars. News of the fall of Constantinople in 1453 had awakened new zeal, leading to several small and unsuccessful ventures in the later 1450s. Ferdinand and Isabella were keen to do the job properly and finish *Reconquista* for good. For a deeply devout Christian like Isabella, it was part of a huge and almost mystical enterprise. After the fall of Granada, she hoped to continue the battle into Africa, then across the Atlantic, and eventually to Jerusalem.

It took ten years to complete the conquest of Granada. Although Castile provided the bulk of the manpower, Aragon contributed money, ships and supplies as well as troops. The best artillery was provided, which meant that siege operations were over swiftly. Cavalry were of little use in such mountainous country, so the infantry were trained and toughened and new strategies developed. This laid the foundations for the emergence of the Spanish infantry as the most effective fighting force in Europe in the following century.

Ferdinand and Isabella had won the pope's blessing for their enterprise; this meant they could levy a tax on the clergy, the *cruzada*, to help pay for it. The pope also gave them a huge silver cross which was always held aloft during sieges and attacks, and this features prominently in paintings of these battles. Ferdinand and Isabella's success was also helped by divisions among their enemies. The aged and ineffective king of Granada, Mulay Hassan, quarrelled with his own son, Boabdil. Boabdil became an ally of Spain, negotiating the surrender of Granada in exchange for the right to keep several other towns. By 1485, Mulay Hassan's brother, El Zagal, had become king, and was willing to co-operate in this deal. Treacherous once again, Boabdil changed sides at the eleventh hour and decided to fight for the city of Granada after all.

The king and queen came in person to lead the last stages of the campaign, the siege of the town of Granada itself, with its marvellous complex of administrative buildings and its palace, the Alhambra. Disheartened by the huge army encamped at their gates, the Muslim leaders chose negotiation and surrender rather than a fight to the end, and the Spanish forces entered the city in January 1492. Announcing the news to their subjects, the king and queen wrote, 'We assure you that this city of Granada is greater in population than you can imagine; the royal palace very grand and the richest in Spain'. They also sent the news with great pride to their fellow monarchs, delighting in the boost to their prestige that this victory gave them.

The aftermath

The victors were generous; the Muslims were allowed to keep their own religion and customs, and their own local government officers. The crown acquired very little land; the big rewards went to a few magnate families, in spite of decrees limiting the acreage that any individual could take.

Moderation and tolerance did not last long. The first archbishop of Granada, Talavera, was deeply interested in Muslim culture, but his policy of gradual conversion and assimilation was viewed with impatience by many. Cisneros, archbishop of Toledo, visited Granada with Ferdinand and Isabella in 1499, and persuaded them to reverse this liberal policy. Christianity was forced on the Muslims, producing large numbers of nominal converts but also a revolt in that year. Ferdinand crushed this and told those who refused to convert that they must emigrate. Outward conformity, secret Islamic practices and a fund of resentment were the outcome. Like the Jews, before they were expelled in 1492, the Muslims remained in Spain on sufferance, undervalued for their great contribution to the country's economic and cultural life, and vulnerable to being thrown out when the government thought the time was ripe. Once Granada had fallen, there was a call to carry forward the crusade against the Muslims into North Africa. Again the pope gave the enterprise his blessing, but war in Italy kept Spanish soldiers occupied for some years. Isabella made a deathbed request that it should be undertaken, and, a year later, in 1505, Cardinal Cisneros led an expedition that captured Oran. He hoped to be encouraged to go further and establish Spanish control far into the south; but Ferdinand favoured occupying only a few key points along the coast of North Africa, wishing to keep troops free for his Italian ventures. It turned out to be the wrong decision; pirates sought out safe bases away from the Spaniards' reach, from which, for many years, they harried Mediterranean merchant ships.

Columbus and the expansion westwards

In 1492, the same year in which Granada fell, Christopher Columbus set sail westwards to find a new route to the Indies. The Genoese mariner had approached the king and queen (and several other possible sponsors) with his proposal several years earlier, but there was no money to spare until victory over Granada was in sight. Columbus was careful to maintain his connections with the queen, and was granted audiences with Isabella in 1489 and 1491.

He made maximum use of these occasions to spin a wonderful web of promises and half-truths about his and others' experiences on the oceans of the world. Knowing of the queen's deep piety, he took care to stress the religious as well as the financial and political dividends his success would bring to Castile. Ferdinand and Isabella were promised that profits from his voyage would help finance a crusade to Jerusalem, and he agreed to take on board a converted Jew with a knowledge of Arabic to explain Christianity to the heathens of the East. The king and queen were by now keen to back an explorer promising a new trade route to the East that was outside Portugal's control, for Portuguese explorers were penetrating further and further south along the African coast at this time, hoping to open up a sea passage to the spices of the East Indies. Columbus expected to reach China or Japan by sailing westwards, but he also believed there was a chance of finding unexplored islands. He agreed with the king and queen that he would take possession of any new lands in their name but, at that stage, there was no thought of permanent settlement.

In March 1493, Columbus returned from his first voyage across the Atlantic and hurried to send news to Ferdinand and Isabella. They summoned him to Barcelona, where he told them of the seven islands he had found, and showed them gold, cotton and cinnamon, and also six native men 'the colour of cooked quinces'. They urged him to set off quickly on a second voyage with far greater resources. He persisted in his claim to have reached the Indies, but conceded that he had discovered unknown islands as well. Ferdinand and Isabella wanted him to claim further new territories for Spain and to make a real landfall in Asia. At that time, the geographical reality of his voyage was still not appreciated.

Rivalry with the Portuguese

The discovery of new lands opened up the likelihood of further rivalry with the Portuguese, who were still hoping to find a new southern trade route to Asia. In 1493, Pope Alexander VI had issued a bull confirming the status of the newly discovered lands as a papal fief held by the Spanish crown, and marking out separate spheres of influence for Spain and Portugal. Next year, the two countries formally ratified the agreement by the Treaty of Tordesillas; the demarcation line was drawn 370 leagues (about 2,050 kilometres) west of the Cape Verde Islands. Spain had the rights to all lands discovered beyond the line and Portugal to lands found east of the line (which eventually gave her Brazil). The equivalent eastern line, halfway round the globe, remained unfixed for nearly a century. Because no one realised the true extent of the American continent, the full implication of the agreement reached between the two countries was not fully understood.

Conflicting aims in the Americas

The unforeseen outcome of the voyage west, the discovery and acquisition of Central and South America, provided a new outlet for the energy which had built up in response to the campaign for the conquest of Granada. The younger sons and poverty-stricken *hidalgos* found here the lands and the riches they still sought; the church was provided with thousands of potential Christians (the American Indians proved easier to convert than the Muslims). In retrospect, Spain was the country most likely to start the process of European colonisation. After 1492, the surplus national drive and energy provided plenty of ambitious and foot-loose adventurers and settlers. She also had experienced boat-builders and deep-sea fishermen to provide mariners and expert navigators, and long experience in overseas trade from Seville and the ports of Catalonia. She also controlled the Canary Islands as a convenient staging post in the Atlantic.

Columbus had never envisaged establishing a permanent settlement; he had sailed west in the expectation of reaching Asia, and in the hope of establishing trading posts and a new route by which precious spices could reach Europe. It soon became clear, however, that there were several very different visions of how Spain and her new colonies across the Atlantic should relate to one another. The crown believed it had a duty to support the church in bringing Christianity to the new lands; it wanted to keep tight control there to protect its new subjects and also ensure that a portion of any profits went to the royal coffers. Columbus' main objectives were to build up trade, to get rich and to acquire noble status; Ferdinand and Isabella were promised that any new lands would be claimed for Castile, and, in return, Columbus was granted the title of Grand Admiral and one tenth of all goods exported from these lands.

The adventurers and newly pardoned criminals who sailed with him had different aims. They were obsessed with tales of gold, and wanted only to get rich as quickly as possible. They were soon followed by a future group, the settlers, who wanted land and cheap labour to work it. Inevitably, the differing aims of all the interested parties led to conflict, and Columbus himself was a victim of this (his mismanagement as Governor of Hispaniola led to disgrace and temporary imprisonment). Long afterwards, historians wrongly accused him of having introduced the *encomienda*, the system that gave Spanish settlers the right to exploit the labour of whole communities of Indians in return for an obligation to teach them Christianity and give military service. It now seems more probable that Columbus gave grants of land that had a limited right of local labour attached (*repartimentos*). Both systems were closely entwined and developed into near-slavery. These practices were bitterly opposed by missionaries who campaigned successfully against them.

Columbus' achievements and their impact on Spain

In the course of his four voyages, Columbus discovered not only the West Indies, but also part of the American mainland. By the time he died, in 1506, permanent settlement in the West Indies had begun, and Seville's monopoly through the House of Trade had been established (see page 34). No one in Spain yet appreciated the tremendous scale of what would become New Spain, Castile's territories across the Atlantic, or the impact it would have on the mother country.

New Spain reinforced Castile as the dominant partner of the two kingdoms, and sharpened the economic divisions between them. Yet Isabella did not mention the discovery of the New World in her list of achievements, nor were they inscribed on her tomb. The next great chapter in Spanish colonisation, the conquistadors' capture of the Aztec and Inca empires, came in the following reign.

Relations with European countries

The conquest of Granada and the support of Columbus' voyages were undertaken by Ferdinand and Isabella as equal partners. Foreign policy, in the form of relations with other European countries, was in Ferdinand's hands alone, as had been arranged by the Agreement of Segovia in 1475. Ferdinand never went to war for the sake of it; diplomacy was his preferred way of achieving his objectives. His relish for intrigue, his willingness to be flexible and his skill at manipulating people all contributed to the style of foreign policy which he conducted, while Isabella's much more straightforward and moralistic approach to affairs was less suited to the half-lit world of Renaissance foreign relations.

Aragon had a much longer tradition of involvement with other countries and greater diplomatic expertise than Castile. She had a long frontier with France and her ports faced eastwards across the Mediterranean; Castile was far more isolated. Ferdinand's grandfather had been king of Sicily, Sardinia and Naples as well as Aragon. Although the three countries had since come under different monarchs, they were still ruled by cousins, and Ferdinand inherited an ambition to restore and spread Aragon's power in Italy. Ferdinand had also inherited a tradition of hostility towards France, while Castile had often been an ally of her northern neighbour. Aragon had suffered at the hands of expansionist French kings in the fifteenth century, losing Navarre, Cerdagne and Roussillon along her Pyrenean border.

The early years

In the early years of Ferdinand and Isabella's rule, there was too much to occupy them within Castile and Aragon, and then in Granada, to leave them any resources for an ambitious foreign policy. Yet Ferdinand was able, during that time, to persuade Portugal to renounce her rights to the Canary Islands and agree to the marriage of Prince Alfonso to Princess Isabella (eldest daughter of the Catholic king and queen). Another proposed marriage alliance was that between Spain and the Holy Roman Empire, with the sons and daughters of the two royal families being promised in a double marriage knot. In order to wean Castile from her French friendship, Ferdinand arranged yet another betrothal, this time between his daughter Catherine and Prince Arthur of England, by the Treaty of Medina del Campo in 1489. England and Spain also agreed to launch a double invasion of France. This came to nothing, but the marriage of Catherine and Arthur took place as soon as the pair were old enough and, when Arthur died, Catherine married his younger brother, King Henry VIII. Similarly, Isabella had a second Portuguese husband when the first one died, and her younger sister replaced her as his wife after Isabella's own early death. In this way, the royal children were put into service to cement their parents' alliances.

The Holy League

Ferdinand's next success did not come through his own initiative. Charles VIII of France was planning to invade Italy, and wanted to ensure Spain's neutrality. He agreed to restore Cerdagne and Roussillon as the price, but when the French armies marched on south from Milan and captured Naples in 1495, Ferdinand could not remain neutral. He strongly disputed Charles's claim to rule Naples, where his sister was married to King Ferrante. The first action he took was to revive the now dormant Holy League, which had been formed to protect Italy against foreign invasion. The papacy, the Holy Roman Empire and England joined. (The Emperor Maximilian had just signed the wedding contract between his children and the Spanish prince and princess.)

Diplomatic contacts

Each of these potential allies had first been approached by envoys sent out by Ferdinand. He had already used skilled diplomats in his earlier search for allies; at least two of these men, in England and Austria, had stayed on to become the equivalent of ambassadors. By 1495, Ferdinand had five such permanent representatives, in Rome, Venice, London, Brussels and at the migratory Austrian court. He saw each embassy as a link in the chain by which he was encircling France; it was a great triumph for him when these powers signed the Treaty of Venice in 1495, with the aim of restoring Naples' independence and excluding the French permanently from Italy. Although the Italian city states had been exchanging diplomatic missions for many years, Ferdinand was the first ruler outside Italy to build a network of embassies. It gave him a unique source of information and contacts. If he had possessed a fixed capital, he could have made even greater use of these reports. In fact, they often got lost, as the great trunks of documents tended to get left at whichever royal palace they happened to reach once they were filled to the lid.

Acquisitions in southern Italy

Once Granada was conquered, Ferdinand had a well-tried army at his disposal and could follow diplomacy with military action. Spain's top general, de Córdoba, was sent to southern Italy in 1495, and was able to defeat the now weary French. Several years of intermittent war followed, during which the Spanish troops further developed the fighting methods they had successfully used against the Muslims. By strengthening their fire-power as well as their tactics, they were proving themselves to be the best troops in Europe. For a while, the French and Spaniards agreed that each should occupy half of the kingdom of Naples (which included Sicily and Sardinia) but the settlement did not last. The Spaniards drove out the French, defeating them at the Battle of Cerignola in 1503, and then forcing them to recognise Spanish sovereignty over all three territories. Sicily, Sardinia and Naples were to be administered by the Council of Aragon, and Ferdinand sent viceroys to each territory. The acquisition of these territories brought Spain extra revenue and a new source of food supplies, but it also took her interests eastwards far into the Mediterranean and into potential conflict with the most powerful of all Muslims, the Turks.

The effects of Isabella's death

Isabella's death in 1504 resulted in frantic negotiations between the courts of Castile and Burgundy, where Philip and Juana eagerly awaited the time when they could enjoy their inheritance. Castile and Burgundy were closely linked through the wool trade: nearly half of the two kingdoms' cloth exports went to the Netherlands, while the Netherlands sent a third of her own exports in return. Netherlands merchants were also keen to get a foothold in the new trade with the recently discovered lands over the Atlantic.

Castilian nobles who had suffered under Ferdinand and Isabella's policies were keen to ingratiate themselves with Philip as the up-and-coming ruler. As a precaution, Ferdinand approached Burgundy's traditional enemy, France, signing the Treaty of Blois with Louis XII in 1505. By its terms, Louis renounced his claim to Naples, and Ferdinand was to marry the French king's niece Germaine de Foix; he hoped she might bear a child who would inherit Aragon. (Juana would only rule Castile; if this child had survived, the Union of the Crowns would have been undone again.)

Philip and Juana's arrival in Castile meant that Ferdinand was forced to hand over the government of Castile and retire to Aragon. In fact, he went further, sailing to Naples and dismissing the Castilian governor and any Castilian officials under him. Although Philip's sudden death in 1506 led to Ferdinand's re-instatement as administrator of Castile, he left day-to-day rule to Cardinal Cisneros, and devoted most of his attention to Italy. Here his task, as before, was to consolidate Aragonese control and to prevent a fresh onslaught by the French. He also began to seek a general European peace which would give him the chance to realise the ambition of leading a crusade to conquer Egypt and win Jerusalem. His years of patient diplomacy had taught him the value of backing a winning side; he put this judgement to good use in joining the League of Cambrai against Venice in 1508, which gained him several Adriatic ports on Naples' behalf.

Navarre

In his old age, Ferdinand also sought to realise an ambition far closer to home: the acquisition of the kingdom of Navarre on Aragon's border with France. In his father's reign, it had belonged to Aragon. Ferdinand had recently revived the anti-French Holy League. Now, on the pretext that the ruling Albret family was planning a joint invasion of Castile with French troops, Ferdinand sent an army under the duke of Alba to occupy Navarre in 1512. After a brief period as part of Aragon, it was finally incorporated into Castile in 1515, neatly rounding out Spain's territories up to the Pyrenees.

England

In his last years, Ferdinand also cultivated his friendship with England. His daughter Catherine's marriage to Arthur had ended with the prince's death in 1503 but, after some hesitation, it was decided that she should remain in England and become the bride of Arthur's younger brother, Henry, as soon as he reached adulthood. There were further delays, during which Henry VII briefly considered an alliance with Philip instead, but the marriage finally took place in 1509. By then, another marriage alliance had been planned, between Henry VII's daughter Mary and Philip's heir Charles.

Ferdinand's achievements

Marriage alliances, like much of Ferdinand's foreign policy, were designed to act as a barrier to French expansion. By the time he died, Ferdinand had built up a chain of allies or potential allies against France: England, the Empire and the Netherlands, as well as Spain itself. He had also extended Spain's frontiers to include the whole of the Iberian peninsula apart from Portugal. When Ferdinand's grandson, Charles, became king of Aragon as well as Castile in 1516, he inherited his grandfather's hostility to France and his determination to protect his interests in Italy against French encroachment. He also inherited the diplomatic network that Ferdinand had created. In the long run, however, the most significant developments in Spain's foreign policy in the years 1474 to 1516 were the acquisition of Naples and Sicily, and above all the expansion into the New World.

Document case studies

The conquest of Granada

2.1 Ferdinand and Isabella's terms before the surrender of Granada

A letter of 28 November 1491 sent to the Moorish king, quoted by Luis de Marmol Carajal in his Historia del rebelión y castigo de los Moriscos del reino de Granada, *1600*

First the Moorish king . . . officials and other leaders, and the entire population of the city of Granada . . . shall within forty days surrender to their Highnesses . . . All will be allowed to remain in their homes and estates, now and for all time . . . Their Highnesses shall forever permit . . . all the population to live by their own law . . . No person shall be allowed to maltreat by word or deed those Christians who have become Moors . . .

Neither shall any Moors be compelled to become Christian against their will.

Source: Englander, Norman, O'Day and Owens (eds.), *Culture and belief in Europe, 1450–1600*, London, 1990

2.2 Promises made to the inhabitants of Granada

Extract from the Capitulations *of 1491, summarised in the contemporary Arabic chronicle of the Nazaritas kings,* Nubhdat al-asr

Of the Capitulations agreed between the people of Granada and the King of the Christians there were:

A promise of security for themselves and their townships and womenfolk and children and cattle and homes and gardens and farms and all possessions.

Source: L. P. Harvey, *Islamic Spain*, Chicago, 1990

2.3 Terms agreed on the surrender of Granada

Extract from the Castilian version of the Capitulations*, 1492*

6. Their highnesses [Ferdinand and Isabella] and their successors will ever afterwards allow King Abi Abdilehi and his judges . . . military leaders . . . and good men, and all the common people, great or small, to live in their own religion, and not permit their mosques to be taken from them.
7. The Moors shall be judged in their laws and law-suits according to the code . . . which it is their custom to respect, under the jurisdiction of their judges.

L. P. Harvey, *Islamic Spain*, Chicago, 1990

2.4 Alonso de Santa Cruz on the intentions of Cisneros, archbishop of Toledo

From Alonso de Santa Cruz's Chronicle of the Catholic monarchs

The archbishop of Toledo wished to remain in Granada [in 1499] with the zealous desire and intention of trying to see if he could convert the Moors to the faith of Jesus Christ, and if he could not, at least of seeing to it that those who were of Christian descent should be converted . . . those converted . . . were given assistance by him; those who refused, he had put in prison. As this affected many Moors, there was a great outcry.

Source: L. P. Harvey, *Islamic Spain*, Chicago, 1990

2.5 Yuce Banegas on the conquest of Granada

Yuce Banegas, member of a distinguished family from Granada, as quoted by a Morisco author who visited him

My son: I am quite aware that you know little of the things of Granada, but do not be surprised if I recall them, for there is not a moment when it does not all reverberate in my heart . . . Do not doubt what I say, because . . . with my own eyes I saw all the noble ladies, widows and married, subjected to mockery, and I saw more than three hundred maidens sold at public auction. I lost three sons, all of them died in defence of the religion, and I lost two daughters and my wife.

Source: L. P. Harvey, *Islamic Spain*, Chicago, 1990

Document case-study questions

1 What is 'the religion' referred to in 2.3?

2 In what circumstances was the letter in 2.1 sent, and does its tone make it effective for its purpose?

3 In which respects did the *Capitulations*, as recorded in 2.2 and 2.3 fulfil the promises made in 2.1?

4 How far did the treatment of the Moors in the years following 1492 fulfil the promises in the letter and the *Capitulations*? Use the documents and your own knowledge.

5 Would you judge the author of 2.5 to be an impartial and reliable witness? Give your reasons.

6 What was the outcome of Cisneros's conversion efforts, and how did these contrast with his predecessor's methods?

Columbus and Spanish–Portuguese rivalry

2.6 Isabella and Christopher Columbus

Isabella to Christopher Columbus, September 1493 (letter)

Dom Cristobal Colon, my Admiral of the Ocean Sea, Viceroy and Governor of the islands newly discovered in the Indies. With this messenger I send you a copy of the book which you left here, which has been so long delayed because it has been made secretly so that the Portuguese emissaries here should not know of it, nor anyone else . . . Certainly, according to what has been said and seen in the present negotiations here, we know increasingly from day-to-day the importance, greatness, and substantial nature of the business, and that you have served us well therein . . . you will receive from us much more honour, grace and increase, as is right and as your services and merits deserve. The sea chart which you have to make you will send me when it is finished . . . In the Portuguese negotiations nothing has been decided with the envoys who are here.

Source: F. Fernandez-Armesto, *Columbus*, Oxford, 1991

2.7 Isabella and Columbus

Isabella to Columbus, August 1494 (letter)

Since matters with Portugal are now agreed, ships can come and go in perfect safety . . . An arrangement has been made with my ambassadors and on the question of the demarcation line or boundary which has still to be made, because it seems to us a problem of great difficulty, we should like you, if possible, to play a part in the negotiations.

Source: F. Fernandez-Armesto, *Columbus*, Oxford, 1991

2.8 Isabella and Columbus

Columbus to Isabella, probably late 1499 or early 1500 (undated letter)

The land which God has newly given your Highnesses on this voyage must be reckoned continental in extent, wherein your Highnesses must take great joy and render Him infinite thanks, and abhor them who say that you should not spend money on this enterprise, for they are not friends of the honour of your high estate – to say nothing of the souls for whose salvation we can hope, whereof your Highnesses are cause, and which is our chief gain.

Source: F. Fernandez-Armesto, *Columbus*, Oxford, 1991

2.9 Columbus proposes a meeting with Vasco da Gama

Isabella's reply to Columbus, 1502 (letter). Vasco da Gama was currently on his second voyage round the Cape of Good Hope to India. Columbus believed he could sail on westwards from his newly discovered lands and link up with da Gama in the Far East.

And in respect to what you say about Portugal, we have written appropriately to the King of Portugal, our son-in-law, and send you herewith the letter addressed to his captain, as requested by you, wherein we notify him of your departure towards the west, and say we have learned of his departure eastward, and that if you meet on the way you are to treat each other as friends.

Source: F. Fernandez-Armesto, *Columbus*, Oxford, 1991

Document case-study questions

6 Explain the word 'increase' as it is used in 2.6 and the phrase 'continental in extent' in the context of 2.8.

7 What was the name of the treaty made between Spain and Portugal in the interval between 2.6 and 2.7 and why was it thought necessary?

8 Why was an accurate sea-chart essential for the negotiation of this treaty, and why was it so difficult to make at this date?

9 What opposition to Columbus' exploration is revealed in 2.8 and how does Columbus justify his voyages?

10 Contrast the Spanish attitude towards Portugal shown in 2.6 and 2.9 and explain why this had come about.

11 What do these documents reveal about the relationship between Columbus and his royal patrons, and how far does the impression given here reflect the changes which that relationship underwent?

3 Charles V: the Netherlands and Spain

Charles's character and upbringing

Erasmus, the great humanist scholar, wrote that he wanted a prince both glorious and of flawless integrity. These words come in *The institution of a Christian prince*, the book he intended as a guide for the fifteen-year-old Charles, who already ruled the Netherlands, and was shortly to add Spain and the Holy Roman Empire to his responsibilities.

These were high aspirations for the shy, unprepossessing youth with a prominent lower jaw, who had become ruler of the Netherlands on his father, Philip's, death in 1506. His mother, Juana, was mentally unstable; widowhood drove her over the brink to insanity. She and Charles's younger brother, Ferdinand, remained in her native land of Spain while Charles and his sisters were brought up by their aunt, Margaret of Burgundy, in the Netherlands. Here, at least, the 'glorious' part of Erasmus' hopes were fulfilled, as the Burgundian court at Brussels was among the most splendid in Europe. Charles grew up among rich tapestries and paintings, in a palace where an elaborate late-medieval formality still governed behaviour. All the great nobles belonged to the Order of the Golden Fleece, sharing a knightly code and considering themselves of equal importance to the prince.

Besides Charles's aunt, the closest influences on him were his tutor, Adrian of Utrecht, who instilled a deep piety in his pupil, and his politically astute Governor, the Grand Chamberlain, Chièvres. Between them, they taught him that it was his duty to defend the Christian faith, and to do all in his power to extend the influence of his family, the Habsburgs. Erasmus' manual for the prince emphasised the obligation to rule according to Christian morality, and also to seek peace at all times. The impact of all these influences can be seen during his reign; but in his youth Charles preferred jousting to study. He thought and spoke slowly, and took a long time to make up his mind when alternative proposals were put to him. Added to his inexperience, this meant that he was still dependent on his mentors when he was declared to be old enough to take over as ruler of the Netherlands in 1515, and to become king of Spain on the death of his grandfather, Ferdinand of Aragon, in 1516.

The Spanish inheritance

Charles's first visit to Spain

One year later, in 1517, the young king and his advisers set sail from Flushing for Spain, but trouble was already in store for him. Chièvres had started to give lucrative positions to his friends and relations, alienating the Spaniards. No one

The humanist Erasmus, painted by Hans Holbein the Younger in 1523.

had thought of encouraging Charles to learn to speak Spanish. He appeared wholly foreign to his new subjects, and they preferred his younger brother Ferdinand, who had been brought up in Spain. Chièvres had this potential rival promptly removed to the Netherlands, barely giving the brothers time to meet each other. The old archbishop, Cardinal Cisneros, who had been running the country since Ferdinand's death, waited to meet Charles. Instead he received a letter of dismissal (drafted by Chièvres, who feared that Cisneros would support Ferdinand) and died that very day.

Charles was too young and inexperienced to curb his Flemish advisers' greed, as they plundered Spanish treasures and took over more and more jobs. Chièvres even made his sixteen-year-old nephew archbishop of Toledo, and the presidency of the *Cortes* of Castile (called to swear allegiance to Charles and grant him money), was given to a Netherlander. The *Cortes* of Aragon and Catalonia needed even tougher persuasion before they acknowledged Charles as king and granted him money.

As resentments multiplied, news reached Spain that Charles's grandfather Maximilian had died. At once all the young man's attention was focused on becoming elected as Holy Roman Emperor. While Charles saw the Empire as a prestigious prize, and a way in which his scattered territories could be given a central focus, the Spaniards regarded it with suspicion. They realised it would take Charles away from Spain for long periods and lead to demands for money. They also saw that, if interests clashed, it would always be the Empire that took priority. Already, on hearing the news, Charles had summoned the *Cortes* of Castile to remote Santiago to ask for money to pay for his journey to Germany. When he sailed from Spain, in May 1520, with Adrian of Utrecht left as regent, the country was on the brink of revolt.

The *Comunero* and the *Germanias* revolts

While Charles was successfully bribing the electors and winning the Imperial throne, the inhabitants of Toledo, and then of other cities in northern Castile rose up in what is known as the *Comunero* revolt. Its most obvious cause was resentment at rule and exploitation by foreigners; but it was also the result of the towns losing their authority over many years, as the central government became more effective. As the revolt took hold, the *corregidors* were chased away and communes established in many towns. Delegates met to send a list of demands to Charles, which included greater independence for the *Cortes*, as well as the removal of foreign officials.

Charles hoped to bring peace by a series of concessions that would give Spaniards a share in the regency, and by suspending the collection of special taxes. This did not satisfy all the rebels, but by now the growing violence and the emergence of more extreme demands sent many nobles back to supporting the government. In 1521, the royal army defeated the rebels at the Battle of Villalar and three of the rebel leaders were executed.

Meanwhile a separate revolt, known as the *Germanias*, broke out in Valencia and Mallorca. Here, the motives were social and economic, the have-nots against

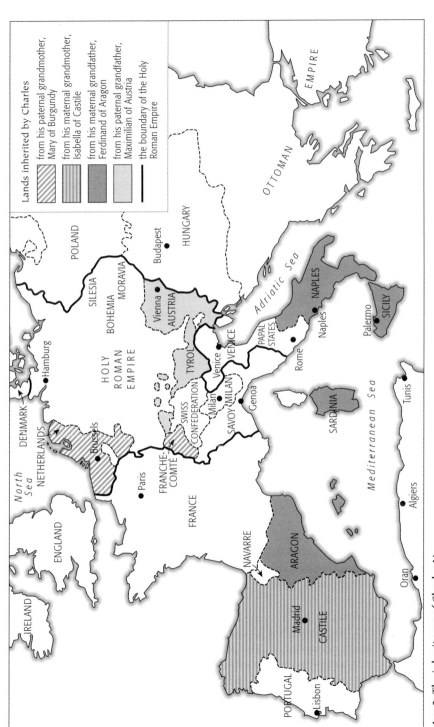

Map 2. The inheritance of Charles V.

Lands inherited by Charles

from his paternal grandmother, Mary of Burgundy

from his maternal grandmother, Isabella of Castile

from his maternal grandfather, Ferdinand of Aragon

from his paternal grandfather, Maximilian of Austria

the boundary of the Holy Roman Empire

North Sea

IRELAND

ENGLAND

DENMARK

Hamburg

NETHERLANDS

Brussels

Paris

FRANCE

FRANCHE-COMTÉ

POLAND

SILESIA

BOHEMIA

MORAVIA

HOLY ROMAN EMPIRE

Vienna AUSTRIA

TYROL

SWISS CONFEDERATION

Milan

SAVOY

Genoa

Venice VENICE

PAPAL STATES

Rome

Budapest

HUNGARY

Adriatic Sea

OTTOMAN EMPIRE

NAPLES

Naples

SICILY

Palermo

SARDINIA

Mediterranean Sea

Tunis

Algiers

Oran

NAVARRE

ARAGON

Madrid

CASTILE

PORTUGAL

Lisbon

the haves, although the rebels had the political aim of establishing a republic on the lines of Genoa. Here, too, the support of more influential people was lost as the extreme elements gained power. Government forces were victorious by 1521, and again the leaders were punished while the followers were pardoned.

The Netherlands: consolidating control

The rebellions in Spain had made Charles realise that his presence was needed there. A pattern was now set that continued throughout his reign: he always tried to be in that part of his many dominions where he was most needed.

First, however, he spent a year in the Netherlands from 1521 to 1522, re-appointing his aunt Margaret as regent. He replaced her with his sister Mary when Margaret died in 1531. He also began a policy of consolidation and, over the next twenty years, he brought a number of component parts of the Netherlands under tighter control. He also acquired several small territories by conquest or confiscation to round out the frontiers. In 1548, the seventeen provinces that made up the Netherlands were formally reorganised into a single political unit, separate from the Holy Roman Empire. Although Charles made great demands on the inhabitants for money, the Netherlands remained stable and loyal throughout his reign. The only exception was the revolt at Ghent in 1539 (see page 36). Charles was careful to respect the nobles' privileges and used his patronage skilfully to retain their support. When Protestant ideas seeped across the border from Germany, they were rigorously suppressed, although by the end of the reign this policy had begun to change.

Spain: extending royal authority

Charles had grown up in the Netherlands, and was to return there for his abdication. It was Spain and Germany, however, which occupied the greater part of his attention throughout his reign. When he left Castile after the *Comunero* revolt, he paid brief visits to England and the Netherlands, and then, in 1520, went on to Aachen to be crowned as king of Germany. From there he moved on to the Diet of Worms to grapple with the problem of Luther (see page 45). He was not free to leave again for Spain until 1522. Once there, he remained for the best part of seven years, making a real effort to be seen as a good Spaniard in his subjects' eyes. He learnt to speak Spanish, married Isabella of Portugal (earlier proposals for a French or English bride had fallen through), and grew genuinely to love the country.

His main effort was devoted to Castile, where the *Cortes* had been weakened by the failure of the *Comunero* revolt. Yet Charles appreciated that genuine grievances underlay the revolt, and was keen to summon Castile's *Cortes* regularly and listen to its petitions. With tactful handling, Castile could be asked to supply the money of which Charles was always in desperate need (although he made sure the *Cortes* was only allowed to discuss its grievances after the cash had been granted). The nobility did not oppose Charles as long as their tax exemption was untouched. It was always the peasants and the middle class who had to pay the *servicios* voted by the *Cortes*. At the same time, Charles realised that there was little point in attempting to squeeze more money out of the more independent *Cortes* of Aragon because they represented such a poor region of Spain.

From now on, Spain remained peaceful, and Charles and his advisers extended the system of government put in place by Ferdinand and Isabella. Each of Charles's dominions, like Spain, was allowed to retain and, in some cases, develop its own administrative machinery; there was no attempt to impose an overall pattern. After Chièvres died in 1521, Mercurino Gattinara, Charles's Chancellor, became his chief adviser. For the next nine years, until his death in 1530, Gattinara encouraged Charles to see all his dominions as part of a coherent whole, but no central institutions were ever created.

The royal councils

The structure of royal councils was, in theory, well-fitted to Charles's and Spain's needs; he was likely to be away for most of the time, and these committees of officials could carry on the business of government in his absence. Their written recommendations could be sent to him for approval. Policy was co-ordinated by Francisco de los Cobos, who had the title of Royal Secretary.

At the apex of this system came the Council of State, but under Charles its functions were mainly formal and he consulted it less and less. The Council of Castile (already in existence, but reorganised early in Charles's reign) was far more powerful. It consisted of on average eight royal officials (grandees were excluded) who were responsible for the day-to-day running of Castile and also acted as a Court of Appeal. The Council of Aragon functioned in a similar way, but it was Castilians who were chosen for the bulk of official posts.

There was a new Council of War, but the two most powerful and innovative creations were the Council of Finance and the Council of the Indies.

The Council of Finance

The Council of Finance, established in 1523, met daily to examine the estimates of income and expenditure and to supervise and control them. At the start, it was only concerned with Castile's finances, but gradually it took over the task of raising the money to pay for Charles's foreign wars. los Cobos started as secretary here before he took over the same job for several of the other councils. Charles did not communicate directly with his councils, whose role was to produce written statements of advice, but through the secretaries. This gave los Cobos much influence with the Emperor; he was the co-ordinator of the various councils, and also the person responsible for appointing and training the growing body of royal officials. For a while, he had to compete for power with the Emperor's Chancellor, Gattinara, but Charles made it plain that los Cobos was in charge within Spain. During the Emperor's long absences, he acted as adviser to the regent, Queen Isabella. Charles, like his grandparents, kept the nobility out of home government; minor gentry and university-trained lawyers and clerics provided the manpower as the organs of government multiplied.

The Council of the Indies

Another new council with enormous power was the Council of the Indies. This had overall charge of the administration, the legal system and the church in all Spain's transatlantic territories. These were, moreover, spectacularly enlarged in Charles's reign by the conquests of Cortés and Pizarro. Its president and eight councillors supervised the men on the spot, the viceroys and the *audiencias*. But, at a time when the voyage across the Atlantic took about two months, problems had often reached a crisis or resolved themselves by the time instructions arrived from Spain. Inevitably, the viceroys, who were Castilian nobles, acquired virtual autonomy.

The Americas

Establishing control

Spain had the task of creating a method of controlling distant overseas territories on a scale far beyond anything demanded in the past. She had no example to follow; no other European nation faced this problem until much later. The system of a council in Spain and viceroys within the territory was also used for Spain's newly acquired lands in Italy. Its aim was to create a balance of power between the men overseas and the controlling body at home. Until the councils began to wilt under the weight of their own bureaucracy, it was able to provide this.

The crown kept close control of the economies of the new colonies through Seville's monopoly of trade. The House of Trade in Seville, founded in 1503, was placed under the supervision of the Council of the Indies as soon as this was set up in 1524.

The crown's policy of confining all shipping across the Atlantic to this one port seems extraordinary today, but it was accepted because of the practical benefits of sending out well-organised fleets, with means of defence against pirates. Seville, moreover, had several geographical advantages over Spain's other ports. The Andalucian hinterland provided the bulk of the grain, wine and oil which was shipped out to feed the settlers and the port had direct access to the Atlantic down the Guadalquivir River. The town boomed, as it was seen as the gateway to Eldorado by enterprising men from all over Spain and beyond; so did the sheep farmers and the wool industry of northern Castile, stimulated by the new market. Food and cloth went across the Atlantic from Seville, and in return a few new products were sent back (including tomatoes), but the bulk of the imports were paid for in precious metals.

Gold and silver was the chief attraction for the thousands of Spaniards who left for the New World. Cortés in Mexico and Pizarro in Peru had been spurred on to their extraordinary feats of conquest by the promise of huge amounts of bullion. They were soon followed by Christian missionaries. Although such men were always a small minority, their influence on royal policy meant that the crown tried to protect the native Americans against ruthless exploitation by the settlers. When gold and silver began to flow across the Atlantic in increasing quantities, the crown laid down that a fifth of all bullion imports should be paid directly into the royal treasury. Clearly this process was much easier to control through one port of entry, Seville.

The impact on Spain's economy

American gold and silver helped to provide the extra cash that Charles needed for his increasingly costly wars. It also enriched many private individuals. But it was a poisoned chalice: in combination with a rising population, the inflow of bullion caused prices to rise in Spain, and then in the rest of Europe. Because Spanish prices rose first, Spanish goods became increasingly uncompetitive. Foreign merchants and manufacturers were able to undercut Spanish prices, and increasingly penetrated the profitable market in the Americas.

To make matters worse, Spanish manufacturers could not match their foreign competitors in quality of goods and speed of delivery. Another area where Spain failed to take advantage of its huge opportunity in the Americas was in the production of grain. The settlers needed this till they could grow their own; so did the rising population in Spain itself. But the peasant farmers were so ground down by high taxes that they could not afford the capital cost of bringing new ground into cultivation. Food prices rose as demand outstripped supply. Meanwhile, crown protection of sheep farming meant that much suitable fertile land could not be cultivated.

As with the task of developing a system of government for distant colonies, Spain had no model to follow in coping with these economic problems. Members of the Council of Finance were officials, not practical businessmen. The government expected them to produce the maximum revenue but was not interested in methods of stimulating the country's economy in general. The true extent of the lost opportunities and the damage was not clearly visible until the reign of Charles's son.

The problems of Charles's last years

The economic crisis

Warning signs of the impending economic crisis were, however, appearing in Charles's last years. He had always been a lavish spender, but the costs of his wars increasingly began to bite in the 1530s and 1540s. By 1534, crown expenditure was more than double income. Government revenues increased by 50 per cent during Charles's reign, but prices went up 100 per cent. Three main sources of income were pushed to the limit. Firstly, there were the taxes provided by Castile, including the *alcabala* (sales tax) and the *cruzada*, which became a regular triennial tax long after its original justification – a crusade – had disappeared. Secondly, there was the crown's share of the bullion imports, which came to be mortgaged further and further in advance to pay interest on annuities (*juros*), which were sold by the government. The third source of income came from bank loans. Most of the banks approached were foreign and, as the chances of repayment receded, so the interest demanded on the loans rose.

Between 1526 and 1539, Charles was away from Spain for three long periods. The Empress Isabella was left in charge, but the heavy responsibility and the loneliness gradually reduced her stamina. She died of influenza after a premature stillbirth in 1539. With no one else available, Charles appointed his twelve-year-old son Philip as regent in his mother's place, with the experienced president of the Council of Castile, Talavera, to advise him.

The Ghent revolt

The Emperor was in a hurry to leave Spain because a revolt had broken out in the Netherlands. The citizens of Ghent had risen against their ruler, the regent, Mary of Hungary (Charles's sister), in protest against the high taxes demanded of them to pay for a war against France. Charles was determined to punish them, and arrived in 1540 accompanied by five thousand German mercenaries. The leaders and a number of others accused of joining in the rebellion were arrested. Torture was used to extract confessions and many were executed. The city was fined and deprived of its privileges. A district of Ghent was pulled down and a fortress erected on the site to make an even greater example of the city.

Multiplying problems

In a pattern of events so often repeated, Charles left the Netherlands on another more urgent mission, before the question of its long-term future had been properly resolved. By this stage of his reign, the problems were multiplying out of control. He hardly had time to visit Spain again before his final retirement there. Wars against the French and the Turks, and problems in his other territories, absorbed his whole attention. In 1545, Charles's son Philip, encouraged by los Cobos, wrote to his father from Spain that 'with what they pay in other ordinary and extraordinary dues, the common people, who have to pay these taxes, are reduced to such utter misery that many of them walk naked'. Two years later, los Cobos was dead, worn out by the impossible task of satisfying his master's insatiable demands for ever more money. Charles was incapable of cutting expenditure, whether it was on the lavish entertainments given at court or on the far more costly foreign wars.

Abdication, retirement and death

By the mid-1550s, Charles had come to realise that his personal resources were exhausted. The task of ruling such a huge empire had proved to be beyond the strength, both physical and mental, of one man. He was always a 'hands-on' ruler, gathering advice and pondering over it at great length, but always taking the vital decisions himself. From a slow start, he had gained confidence and matured into a statesman of good judgement, better at accommodating to the needs of a changing world than some historians have credited him. Most unusually for that epoch, he decided to abdicate in favour of his son, Philip, and brother, Ferdinand, dividing the responsibilities. He went back to his childhood home, Brussels, for the actual abdication from rule over the Netherlands in October 1555 (in the following months he also abdicated his control of the Holy Roman Empire and Spain). The ceremony took place in the great hall of the castle before a large audience led by his relatives and the members of the Order of the Golden Fleece. Observers were impressed by the intense emotion of the event, with not an eye left dry.

Charles chose to spend his last years in Spain, in a villa attached to the remote monastery of Yuste. Always a deeply religious man, the desire to make his peace with God and prepare for death was an additional motive for leaving the political arena to others. He was already in poor health and, in 1558, he caught malaria and died. Two months later, his daughter-in-law, Mary Tudor, also died, ending the plan that his son Philip would rule over an empire of Spain, England, the Netherlands and the Indies. The previous year Philip had been forced to suspend all payments to his bankers, in effect a declaration of bankruptcy. Even with all his energies devoted to Spain, Philip was to give the country a more rigid and less successful rule than his father achieved.

Document case studies
Charles V's problems in Spain

3.1 The *Comunero* revolt of 1520

A contemporary account

The Communes of Castile began their revolt, but after a good start had a bad ending, and exalted beyond what it had previously been the power of the King whom they desired to abase. They rose in revolt because the King was leaving the realm, because of the *servicios*, because of the foreign regent, because of the large amounts of money which were being taken out of the realm, and because the chief office of the treasury had been given to Chièvres, the archbishopric of Toledo to William de Croy, and knighthoods of the Military Orders to foreigners.

Source: Francisco López de Gómara, *Annals of the Emperor Charles V*, translated by R. B. Merriman, Oxford University Press, 1912

3.2 The Castilian *Cortes* at Valladolid, 1522

Charles V's address to the Cortes

Yesterday I asked you for funds; to-day I want your advice. And since it is the first time I come to you for advice, I expect you to give me good advice. Which seems to you better? That you should grant me the *servicio* at once (for as I promised yesterday and as I promise again to-day, I will not dismiss you until I have provided for all the things that you ask for as they are just and beneficial for the welfare of these kingdoms), and thus make clear that I bestow favours of my own free will? Or that I should first reply to your petitions and thus have it said that I do so in order to obtain your *servicio*?

Source: M. Fernandez Alvarez, *Charles V*, London, 1975

3.3 Charles offers encouragement to Isabella

Charles to his wife Isabella, 20 February 1536 (letter)

Madam, there is no need for us to give way to loneliness and self-pity. Take heart and bear whatever God has in store for us. I hope that all will go well. Look after everything with great attention; keep a careful watch on the frontiers of Navarre as well as those of Roussillon, rally the people and get troops together, and look for money everywhere. If God should bless us with some from Peru, even if it is intended for individuals, we must take advantage of it.

Source: M. Fernandez Alvarez, *Charles V*, London, 1975

3.4 The advice of the royal secretary, Francisco de los Cobos

los Cobos to Charles, 1546 (letter)

Remember the importance of finding a remedy for the relief of these kingdoms, because of the extreme need, for otherwise there could not fail to be serious trouble, because the need is so notorious that not only are the natives of the kingdom aware of it and are refusing to take part in any financial transaction, but even foreigners . . . are doing the same thing, because they know there is no source from which payments can be made.

Source: *Calendar of letters, despatches and state papers, Spanish (1485–1558)*, London, 1862–1954

Document case-study questions

1 Explain the term '*servicio*' in Documents 3.1 and 3.2.

2 Why does Charles urge Isabella to 'keep a careful watch on the frontiers of Navarre' and why is this her responsibility in 3.3?

3 How far is the prediction of the author of 3.1 of an increase in royal power shown to have been fulfilled in 3.2?

4 The author of 3.1 cites the king's absence as one of the causes of the *Comunero* revolt. What clues are provided in these documents to explain why Charles had no fear of revolt when he left Spain later, as in 3.3?

5 Show the different ways in which money is a common theme of all four documents, and explain why a shortage of income was a growing problem throughout Charles's reign.

Relations with the New World

3.5 Trade with the Americas and bullion imports

Total imports of treasure in ducats by 5-year periods

Period	Royal	Private	Total
1503–5	116,660	328,607	445,266
1506–10	256,625	722,859	979,484
1511–15	375,882	1,058,782	1,434,664
1516–20	312,261	879,575	1,191,836
1521–25	42,183	118,821	161,004
1526–30	326,485	919,640	1,246,124
1531–35	518,833	1,462,445	1,980,277
1536–40	1,621,062	3,104,408	4,725,470
1541–45	909,346	5,035,460	5,944,806
1546–50	1,911,206	4,699,247	6,610,453
1551–55	4,354,208	7,484,429	11,838,637

Based on the table in E. J. Hamilton, *American treasure and the price revolution, 1501–1650*, Cambridge, Massachusetts, 1934

3.6 The merchants of Seville

A description by a Mexican friar, Tomas de Mercado

First they deal in all parts of Christendom and even Barbary. To Flanders they ship wool, oil and wine, and bring therefrom every kind of haberdashery, tapestry and books. To Florence they send cochineal and hides, and bring back strings of gold, brocades, silks, and from all these countries a great quantity of cloth . . . To all the Indies they ship great cargoes of every kind of merchandise, and return with gold, silver, pearls, cochineal and hides in great quantities. Finally, to insure their cargoes (which are worth millions) they have to take out insurances in Lisbon, Burgos, Lyons and Flanders, because so vast are their shipments that neither the merchants of Seville nor of twenty cities like Seville are capable of insuring them.

Source: J. Lynch, *Spain under the Habsburgs*, London, 1964

3.7 The conversion of the Indians

From las Casas's treatise, On the Indians, *1552, in which he puts forward 30 propositions explaining why Christian rulers had the right to convert the Indians. As a result of this treatise by las Casas, who was a Dominican missionary, the Council of the Indies framed a new legislative code for the New World in 1542.*

Proposition XVIII
The Devil could invent no worse pestilence to destroy all the world and to kill all the people there . . . than the *repartimiento* and *encomienda*, the institution used to distribute and entrust Indians to Spaniards. This was like entrusting the Indians to a gang of devils or delivering herds of cattle to hungry wolves. The *encomienda* or

repartimiento was the most cruel sort of tyranny that can be imagined . . . The Indians were prevented from receiving the Christian faith and religion. The wretched and tyrannical Spanish *encomenderos* [colonists] worked the Indians night and day in the mines and in other personal services. They collected unbelievable tributes . . . I solemnly affirm, as God is my witness, that so long as these *encomiendas* remain, all the authority of the kings, even if they were resident in the Indies, will not be enough to prevent all the Indians from perishing.

Source: Englander, Norman, O'Day and Owens, *Culture and belief in Europe, 1450–1600*, London, 1990

Document case-study questions

6 Explain the distinction between royal and private imports of bullion in 3.5.

7 Explain the terms 'Barbary' in 3.6 and *'repartimiento'* in 3.7.

8 Suggest why there was such a sharp fall in bullion imports between 1521 and 1525, and such a big increase in the 1540s and 1550s.

9 What motive, apart from compassion, would cause the Council of the Indies to act on las Casas's warnings and curb the practice of *repartimiento*? Would las Casas share this motive, or does he reveal another priority in 3.7?

10 With reference to these documents, show the strengths and weaknesses of Spain's overseas trade during Charles V's reign.

4 Charles V as Holy Roman Emperor

The Imperial election

When his grandfather, Maximilian, died in 1519, Charles inherited the Habsburg family lands in central Europe. More importantly, he also made it his objective to win election as the next Holy Roman Emperor. While Maximilian was still alive, he had hoped to have Charles recognised as his heir in advance as 'king of the Romans', avoiding a contested election, but death overtook him before he had accomplished this.

The Imperial crown was a great prize. It gave enormous prestige to its wearer. Hernán Cortés, conqueror of Mexico, writing to tell Charles of his new acquisition in 1524, told him that with this 'there would be nothing more left for your Excellency to do in order to become ruler of the world'. The Holy Roman Empire nominally extended from the Netherlands in the west to Bohemia in the east, and from the Baltic in the north to the Alps in the south. Its head was regarded as the lay head of the Christian world, of equal status to the pope.

In reality, those in charge of the hundreds of sub-divisions that made up the Empire held the real political control. The larger princes had by now consolidated their power and were on the way to becoming rulers of autonomous states. The Emperors' power-base lay in the hereditary lands of the Habsburg family in Austria and southern Germany. Maximilian had concentrated on extending these when his attempts to reform and strengthen the central authority of the Emperor had largely failed.

Having frustrated Maximilian's aims, the princes viewed Charles as his successor with a mixture of hope and apprehension. Since he was already ruler of the Netherlands and Spain, he would bring a greater strength to his position as Emperor than his grandfather ever possessed, and this could be seen as a threat to the pretensions of the individual princes. At the same time, it held out a promise of German national renewal, if an effective central rule could be put in place.

But, first, Charles had to win the Imperial election, and this was by no means a foregone conclusion. Firstly, he had to gain the votes of a majority of the seven electors (the rulers of Saxony, Brandenburg, the Palatinate, Bohemia, Mainz, Trier and Cologne). Also, he faced powerful rivals in Francis I of France and Frederick the Wise of Saxony, with Henry VIII briefly in the contest too.

Charles launched a propaganda campaign to present himself as a true German, ready to defend German liberties and protect Christendom against the

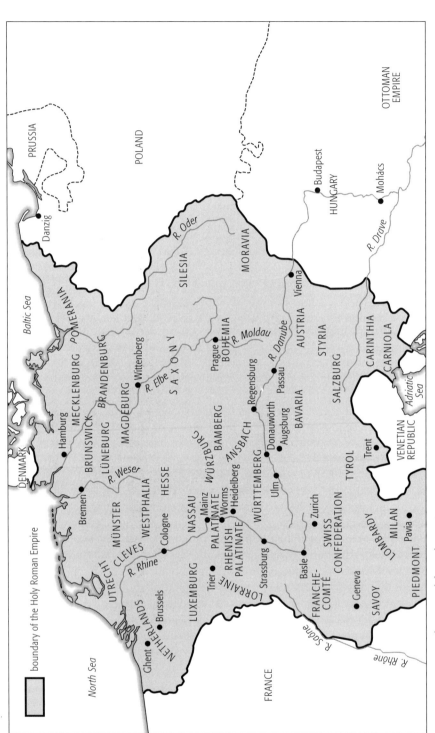

Map 3. Germany at the time of the Reformation.

Turks. Francis was belittled as a foreign adventurer, Frederick the Wise was told he lacked the strength for this latter task. The electors vacillated between one candidate and another, well aware that this would increase the value of their votes. In the end it was bribery that won support for Charles: he could borrow more money than Francis, using the massive resources of the Fugger bank above all. When the vote was finally taken he was elected unanimously.

He also helped his cause by agreeing in advance to a document, known as 'The Capitulation', by which he promised to guarantee to all the German rulers the undisturbed possession of their lands and rights. In addition, he agreed not to bring foreign troops onto German soil, or to declare war without the princes' consent. From that time on, all Emperors had to agree to a similar set of conditions before ascending the throne.

The problems of running the Empire

With his many commitments elsewhere, Charles had to delegate responsibility for the day-to-day running of German affairs to his brother Ferdinand. Not long before, the king of Bohemia and Hungary had promised his daughter Anna as a bride for Ferdinand, but only on condition that his future son-in-law was personal ruler of a substantial territory. Thus two objectives were realised when Ferdinand was named as Charles's regent in Germany and given rule over all the Habsburg family lands in Germany and Austria. This was laid down in the Compact of Brussels of 1522, made on the eve of Charles's return to Spain. The previous year, Ferdinand had married Anna and, eventually, he also became king of Bohemia and Hungary, fulfilling his grandfather's dynastic ambition. Four years later, he acquired another title (promised him in Brussels), that of king of the Romans, assuring him the succession to the Empire after Charles. Thus, in the long run, the Brussels Compact had laid the ground for the eventual division of Charles's inheritance between his Spanish and German possessions.

In 1519, no one realised the full extent of the burden which rule over so many territories would involve. In the event, it was Germany that was to cause Charles the worst troubles. At this date, it consisted of over four hundred separate units, ranging from considerable states such as Saxony to independent towns of all sizes. About a fifth were ruled by prince-bishops, many of them worldly, if not corrupt. The Emperor had nominal authority over all these rulers, but little real control. There was no Imperial army or any effective central administration. Many Germans regretted the divided condition of their country and longed for a national cause. They saw the contrast between Germany's weakness and the growing power of neighbouring nation-states such as France.

One result of this weakness was that no single ruler had the strength to stand up to the demands of Rome. Germans believed they paid far more in papal taxes than people in other countries. Nor had any ruler the authority to compel the church to tackle its corruption, also felt to be worse in Germany than elsewhere. Added to these dissatisfactions, there were the social and economic problems of inland trading cities losing out to the Atlantic ports, and also those of a whole spectrum of groups from the down-trodden peasants to the impoverished minor nobility who were failing to adjust to a changing world. Throughout Germany, many groups existed for whom a new cause would be a welcome means of venting their frustrations and providing fresh hope. In addition, it was Germany which had the greatest proliferation of printing presses in Europe and some of the liveliest humanists. Conditions were ripe for Germany to become the cradle of the Reformation.

The rise of Lutheranism

Martin Luther

By the time Charles was elected Emperor in 1519, the cause that was to become the catalyst of religious change was already in existence. Two years earlier, in Wittenberg, Martin Luther, a German monk and academic, had nailed up his 95 theses attacking the sale of indulgences* on a church door. The city of Wittenberg was ruled by Frederick the Wise of Saxony who had his own reasons for protecting this brilliant theology professor at his university of Wittenberg. The Elector Frederick had, for a time, been the pope's candidate at the Imperial election; he was unlikely to yield to pressure from Charles if Luther was threatened. But, in these early stages of Luther's protest, no one could have foreseen that the attack on well-known corrupt practices could spread to become an onslaught on the foundations of the church itself. In 1517, his message was a demand for reform, not for a breakaway.

Luther's protest was immediately put into print and circulated throughout Germany, causing tremendous excitement. Rome was slow to appreciate the seriousness of the threat posed by this professor in a distant German town, but in 1520 Pope Leo X issued a bull listing Luther's heresies and threatening him with excommunication, unless he recanted within 60 days. He also urged Charles V to take action against this source of danger within his territories.

Luther was encouraged by the growing support given him by his fellow Germans, who saw him as their champion against a greedy and corrupt papacy as well as a theologian with compelling new ideas. Luther, therefore, stuck to his guns. Instead of recanting, he wrote three great pamphlet-manifestos in 1520. These set out his ideas in greater depth, and challenged orthodox Roman Catholic beliefs and practices on many counts. Forgiveness could only be won by faith, not by good works; laymen could read the Bible for themselves, not through a priest as interpreter; the liturgy of the Mass, the central service of the church, should be changed. Over 300,000 copies of these pamphlets were

---

*A 'certificate' granting remission from time in Purgatory. Indulgences were based on the Roman Catholic doctrine that the merits of Christ and the Saints could be drawn on to gain remission of punishment for sin through reduction of time in Purgatory. Originally indulgences were intended to be won by good deeds, but by Luther's time they were often sold. It was against this background that Luther developed his doctrine of Justification by Faith alone, that salvation was won by faith rather than by good works.

printed and distributed throughout Germany, with illiterates crowding to hear them read aloud in towns and villages.

By 1520, Luther and his followers had gone too far to turn back. What had started as a demand for reform of the existing church had developed into full-blown heresy involving the foundation of a new, Lutheran, religion. For the first two years of his campaign, Luther had been protected from punishment by the impending Imperial election; not only was Frederick the Wise a candidate (backed by the pope as a weaker alternative to Charles V), but no one had the authority to take any action in the interim after Maximilian's death. Once he was elected, Charles should at once have tackled this growing crisis in Germany, but the *Comunero* revolt took him to Spain and kept him there till 1521. The only action he had taken so far was to issue a public condemnation of Luther's teachings when the excommunication came into force in January 1521, and to encourage bonfires of heretical books.

The Diet of Worms

It was the Emperor's right to call a Diet, a meeting of all the rulers of the many states which made up the Holy Roman Empire. Charles summoned his subjects to a Diet at Worms in 1521, with the object of introducing himself to them for the first time, and discussing possible political reforms. The problem of Luther was also on the agenda. The actions and beliefs of Luther were abominable to a devout and traditional Christian like Charles. Luther's stand was also a defiant affront to the Emperor's authority and the political as well as religious unity of his lands. Like all contemporary rulers, Charles believed that if his subjects did not all worship the same religion, the state would fall apart. In addition, he believed that Christendom must maintain a united front if it was successfully to withstand the threat of attack from Islam in the east. As Holy Roman Emperor, he was the traditional leader of Christendom, and he took very seriously the implications of this role against both internal and external enemies.

Charles was a man of honour; he also saw the need to conciliate one of his most powerful subjects, the Elector Frederick. Luther was, therefore, invited to come to the Diet to answer in person the accusations of heresy made against him by the pope's representative. He was granted a safe conduct to protect him against a possible summary execution, the fate of John Hus, a heretic summoned to a previous Diet. The Emperor was confident that the awe-inspiring assembly of the Diet would cow Luther into recantation; he also hoped to boost his own reputation by dealing successfully with the threat that Luther posed.

Luther's stand against the Emperor at Worms was not at all what Charles had expected. After a hesitant beginning, the monk from Wittenberg regained courage and made his famous defence of all he had written: 'I cannot and I will not recant anything, for to go against conscience is neither right nor safe.' The earliest printed version adds the famous words: 'Here I stand, I cannot do otherwise.' As a result, the Diet issued its decision to condemn him as a heretic and placed him under its Ban. All members were charged with the task of arresting and punishing him as soon as his safe-conduct had run out. Instead,

Luther before Charles V at the Diet of Worms.

Frederick of Saxony quietly hid him away in a remote castle at Wartburg. Many of the other rulers who had attended the Diet were also unwilling to implement the Ban, and allowed Luther's followers to go on spreading his ideas. In this first major confrontation between Charles and Luther, the Emperor was the loser. While Luther translated the New Testament into German, his followers were organising an independent church and allowing it to come under the control of local princes and town councils.

For eight years after the Diet of Worms, the Emperor was wholly absorbed by conflicts elsewhere, fighting the French and the Turks. Since he needed the German princes' help against these external enemies, Ferdinand (as Charles's regent), was unwilling to antagonise them by demanding that they comply on the Lutheran issue. A number of major German princes converted to Lutheranism during these years; several Diets were summoned, but none had the power to enforce the suppression of Lutheranism. In 1525, the peasants, for a variety of social, economic and religious reasons, rebelled in what became known as the Peasants' War. Luther was horrified by this violent attack on the existing social order, but it did little to prevent the steady spread of Lutheranism. The Diet of Speyer in 1529 managed to lay down that the Worms edict was to be enforced, and that no more church lands were to be taken over by secular authorities, but some members signed a 'Protestation of Disagreement'. It is from this document that the term 'Protestant' derives.

The failure to suppress religious dissent

Charles was forced to reconsider his options. Lacking the military force or the necessary ruthlessness, it was not feasible to deal with Lutheranism by crushing it out of existence. An alternative solution, which greatly appealed to the Emperor, was to persuade the pope to call a General Council to initiate a major reform programme. If that succeeded, he believed that Lutherans would flock back to a cleansed and revitalised Roman Catholic church, and Lutheranism would wither away. He realised that the church had many faults which needed correction, but it was his misfortune that none of the contemporary popes were willing to surrender their authority to a General Council. They also had corrupt practices of their own which they wished to keep private.

Thus the popes were unwilling to co-operate with Charles; so was another group who should have been his natural allies, the German princes who remained loyal to the Roman Catholic church. These men were so fearful of Charles's great power that they were unwilling to do anything which might help to strengthen his position. Yet another peaceful solution also appealed to Charles, the negotiation of a compromise with the Protestants. At the Diet of Augsburg, in 1530, the Protestants presented him with the famous Augsburg Confession, in which the Protestant position was set out in Lutheran terms. Charles responded with the *Confutation*. However, these two documents, which had been drawn up as a basis for discussion, left little hope of any agreement being reached. The Diet ended with the Protestant princes withdrawing and the rump attempting to enforce the Worms edict once more.

Charles was to try these two peaceful solutions, compromise and a General Council, several times in the following years. Brought up on Erasmus' teaching, he always preferred negotiation to confrontation and peace to war. He also continued to need the military and financial help of the German princes in his French and Turkish wars. At the Diet of Nuremberg in 1532, the Protestants were promised toleration until a General Council met, and in return they promised to help Charles fight the Turks.

Yet the more cautious Protestant rulers were well aware that, if he had the force, Charles might attempt to suppress the new religion at any time. They prudently began to organise themselves into the defensive League of Schmalkalden. In the event, Charles was once again plunged into a long period of wars and revolts elsewhere and, during these years, Lutheranism expanded and consolidated. By the time a General Council (the Council of Trent) met, and eventually showed a real determination to bring about reform, it was far too late to achieve Charles's hope of winning back heretics by cleansing the Roman Catholic church.

The Schmalkaldic War and after

A further attempt at constructing a compromise between Lutheran and Catholic practices and beliefs also failed at the Regensburg Diet of 1541. A final attempt took place at the 1546 Diet of Regensburg, but the discussions broke up acrimoniously. Charles found himself driven towards the option he had rejected in earlier years: forceful suppression of Lutheranism. This would involve full-scale war against the Schmalkaldic League. Charles realised that he had a good chance of winning because not all the Protestant princes had joined it. By skilful diplomacy and well-timed bribes, he was able to divide his enemies. Yet, even now, he used force with reluctance; in a letter to his sister (which refers to the 1546 Regensburg Diet) he wrote: 'All my efforts on my journey here, and the Regensburg conference itself, have come to nothing . . . the heretic princes are determined to rise in revolt . . . If we hesitate now we shall lose all . . . force alone will drive them to acceptable terms.' The letter goes on to ask his sister to raise money and troops in the Netherlands for the forthcoming campaign. Further forces were demanded from Italy and Spain; for the moment they were not needed for war elsewhere.

The two armies were evenly matched until one of the Protestant leaders, Maurice of Saxony, defected to the Imperial side with his troops. His reward was to win control of his cousin's lands, the Elector John Frederick of Saxony (nephew of Luther's first patron). This tipped the balance, and Charles's forces were victorious at the Battle of Mühlberg in 1547. The two remaining Protestant leaders were captured and, everywhere Charles's troops passed, Roman Catholic services were restored.

Yet success once again eluded Charles. Lutheranism did not collapse; in large areas of northern Germany it continued to flourish.

At the Diet of Augsburg, later that year, the ever-hopeful Emperor put forward plans for a final solution to Germany's political and religious problems. He proposed to set up a league of all the territories of the Holy Roman Empire with its own council, parliament, court and army. But no one supported him. As usual, the possibility of an effective central organisation sent shivers of fear into every prince, fearful for his own freedom of action. Charles's second proposal, the Augsburg *Interim*, was another attempt to arrive at a compromise solution between Roman Catholic and Lutheran beliefs. This would have maintained the authority of the pope and fundamental Roman Catholic doctrine. However, it went some way towards allowing the Lutheran doctrine of Justification by Faith. and would have allowed priests to marry. It was strongly disliked by both sides, however, and proved to be unenforceable. Charles was unrealistic in hoping that the *Interim* would last until the General Council finally decided on the form of doctrine for the reformed Roman Catholic church. Such a council had been summoned to meet at Trent (technically part of the Holy Roman Empire, although it was just over the border in Italy), but only a few bishops turned up at its opening in 1545. In addition, Pope Paul III remained intensely suspicious of Charles's intentions; he feared that Charles's victory over the Lutherans would make him so powerful that he would try to dictate Rome's policy.

Trouble with the succession

Charles had a further problem in the late 1540s. His brother, Ferdinand, had been named as Charles's successor as Emperor, but Ferdinand now wanted to guarantee that his own son, Maximilian, would succeed him. This provoked Charles to try to secure the right of succession for his own son, Philip, and a bitter family quarrel developed. In 1548 Charles, Ferdinand and Philip met at Augsburg to thrash out a solution. They were soon joined by their sister, Mary, from the Netherlands. Her negotiating skills were well known and Antoine Granvelle wrote to her that: 'Without Your Majesty there is little hope of a successful conclusion.'

By this time, both Ferdinand and his son had become thoroughly naturalised Germans, just as Charles had become a popular ruler in Spain. It was not difficult for the German princes, encouraged by the king of France, to portray Charles as a dictator who was trying to alter the succession plan in order to have a better chance of crushing the liberties of the German people and their rulers. Rumours spread that Philip was planning to replace Ferdinand as Charles's successor as Holy Roman Emperor; in fact these had no foundation. Relations between Charles and Ferdinand became more and more strained as they waited for Maximilian to join the discussions. It was Mary who provided an agreement after months of haggling. Ferdinand was to become Emperor after Charles, to be followed by Philip, who in turn would be succeeded by Maximilian.

The renewal of war

Relations between the Spanish and Austrian branches of the Habsburg family remained sour. Charles had been so absorbed with the succession question that he had failed to notice ominous signs of trouble to come. With two of their leaders still held prisoner after the Battle of Mühlberg, the remaining Protestant princes began to work to avenge their defeat. They realised they needed outside help in order successfully to challenge Charles, and approached the king of France, Henry II. Like his father Francis I, Henry was willing to ally with non-Catholics whenever it was politically expedient. In addition, Maurice of Saxony changed sides once more. He had now been in control of his cousin's lands for some time, but heard rumours that Charles intended to give them back to the Elector John Frederick.

Later that year, the French declared war on Charles and the Protestant princes rose in revolt. Short of troops and money, Charles had to flee to Innsbruck and, even after the arrival of reinforcements from Spain, he could not win back control in Germany. His enemies forced him to accept the Convention of Passau, by which he promised to release the Protestant princes captured at Mühlberg and to allow the Lutherans freedom of worship until a fresh Diet could be called.

The 1555 Diet of Augsburg

The final stage of Charles's manifold attempts to settle the Lutheran problem in fact took place after his abdication. Charles had by now decided to hand over his responsibilities to his brother and son. He could not bear to preside over the 1555 Diet of Augsburg at which all his hopes finally collapsed. By the terms of the peace made at this Diet, the Lutherans were to be allowed freedom of worship in all territories where the ruler supported them. The Latin words describing this settlement are *cuius regio, eius religio*. In cities where both Roman Catholicism and Protestantism were present, they were to exist side by side. Neither side was to seek new converts, and those who did not share their ruler's religion were to be at liberty to move elsewhere.

To the modern observer, this may appear a commonsense solution that should have been reached much earlier. But, in 1555, it was totally revolutionary. In no country had a second religion been tolerated before; it was the action of exhaustion and despair, not of toleration in today's sense. Charles had fought a long struggle to keep religious unity in Germany and, as he had feared, when that failed, the country's political unity was also shattered beyond repair. He left a much-weakened Holy Roman Empire for his brother Ferdinand to rule.

Why did Charles fail?

Charles had consistently underestimated the strength of the Lutherans' religious conviction. This is surprising in a man of such deep personal faith; it was as if he could not believe that anyone would cease to be a Roman Catholic except for ulterior motives – rulers who converted to Lutheranism were, for example, able to confiscate church lands. This is why he was convinced that the Lutherans would abandon large parts of their doctrine and accept his *Interim*, and why he was confident that with their leaders gone, the whole movement would collapse after defeat at Mühlberg.

He failed to understand the many ways in which Luther's teaching appealed to the German people. It gave them a national cause; it provided them with a Bible in rich everyday language, that everyone was encouraged to read and discuss for themselves; it gave the congregations a far more active share in church services, with hymn singing, sermons, and participation in a simpler communion service. Belief in the 'priesthood of all believers' removed the Roman Catholic division between priest and layman and made every member feel he or she was of importance in the new church. Had Luther appeared fifty years earlier, his message could not have been propagated by printed books and pamphlets, many illustrated with crude engravings to bring home their message to those who could not read. But, by the 1520s, Germany had many printing presses and an efficient distribution system. This ensured that Luther's books and pamphlets quickly reached a mass audience.

No one could have stemmed this tide. Charles did his best, and in the end it broke him.

Luther and German nationalism

4.1 The view of Conrad Celtis, a German scholar and humanist

An extract from his address to the University of Ingolstadt, 1492

O men of Germany, assume those ancient passions by which you were so often a dread and terror to the Romans, and turn your eyes to the wants of Germany and consider her lacerated and divided borders. What a shame to have a yoke of servitude imposed on our nation and to pay tributes and taxes to foreign and barbaric kings.

Source: L. W. Spitz (ed.), *The northern Renaissance*, London, 1972

4.2 Resentment against the Roman Curia

Luther's supporter Ulrich von Hutten to the Elector of Saxony, 1520 (letter)

We see that there is no gold and almost no silver in our German land. What little may perhaps be left is drawn away daily by new schemes invented by the council of the most holy members of the Roman Curia . . . what is thus squeezed out of us is put to the most shameful uses . . . a vast number of the worst men are supported in Rome in idle indulgence by means of our money . . . Now if all those who devastate Germany and continue to devour everything might once be driven out, and an end made of the unbridled plundering, swindling and deception with which the Romans have overwhelmed us, we should again have gold and silver in sufficiency and should be able to keep it.

Source: J. H. Robinson, *Readings in European history*, vol. II, London, 1906

4.3 Luther's views on events in Germany

From Luther's 1520 Manifesto, 'To the Christian Nobility of the German Nation Respecting the Reformation of the Christian Estate'

The time for silence is gone, and the time to speak has come . . . The distress and misery that oppress all the Christian estates, more especially in Germany, have led not only myself, but everyone else, to cry aloud and to ask for help, and have now forced me, too to cry out to ask if God would give his Spirit to anyone to reach a hand to his wretched people.

Source: E. G. Rupp and B. Drewery (eds.), 'Martin Luther', in *Documents of modern history*, London, 1970

4.4 The Diet of Worms, April 1521

From Luther's answer before the Emperor

Nobody can deny or dissemble this: the experience and the complaint of all men bear witness that by the laws of the Pope and man-made doctrines, the consciences of the faithful have been most wretchedly ensnared, tormented, tortured; that above all in this renowned German nation, goods and wealth have been devoured by tyranny unbelievable, and to this day the devouring goes on, endlessly and by most grievous means.

Source: E. G. Rupp and B. Drewery (eds.), 'Martin Luther', in *Documents of modern history*, London, 1970

4.5 Luther protests at a proposed new issue of indulgences

Luther to Albert of Mainz, written from Wartburg, December 1521 (letter)

Your Grace has again erected at Halle that idol which robs poor simple Christians of their money and their souls . . . if the idol is not taken down, my duty to godly doctrine and Christian salvation will absolutely force me to attack your Grace publicly as I did the Pope and lay on the Archbishop of Mainz all the odium which Tetzel once had.

Source: E. G. Rupp and B. Drewery (eds.), 'Martin Luther', in *Documents of modern history*, London, 1970

Document case-study questions

1 Explain 'lacerated and divided borders' in 4.1 and 'that idol' in 4.5.

2 Identify Tetzel and the archbishop of Mainz in 4.5.

3 Distinguish between 'Romans' in 4.1 and 'Romans' in 4.2.

4 What similarity of tone do you find between 4.1 and 4.3? Why do you think both writers adopted this style?

5 Suggest why the writers of 4.2 and 4.4 emphasised the economic as well as the moral damage done to Germany by the popes.

6 Use these documents to demonstrate the part played by German nationalism in making the people of Germany so receptive to Luther's ideas.

The election of the Holy Roman Emperors

4.6 A papal official's view

From Francesco Guicciardini's History of Italy, *Book 13, 1536*

There still remained the controversy over the imperial succession, all Christianity looking on with bated breath while both kings put forth their claims more ardently than ever. In this contest, the king of France deceived himself more every day, beguiled by the grand promises of the Marquis of Brandenburg, one of the Electors, who, having received a very great offer of money from him and perhaps a certain amount in down payment, had not only pledged by secret agreements to give him his vote, but promised that his brother, the Archbishop of Mainz, one of the three Prelate Electors, would do the same. The king also anticipated a great deal from another group of Electors, and in case the votes should be even, rested his hope on the ballot of the king of Bohemia. Therefore he sent the Admiral [Guillaume Gouffier, Admiral of France], who had gone to Germany earlier for this election, a very great sum of money to give the Electors.

But the desire of the German people that the Imperial dignity should not be removed from that nation was very great . . . they had begged the Pope not to lend his favour at this election to anyone who was not of German tongue. But the Pope nevertheless continued to favour the king of France, hoping thereby that since he showed himself so ardent in his support, the French king would have to harken with greater trust to his counsels.

And while various disputes were continuing in anticipation of arriving at a decision in due time, an army was put in the field by command of the king of Spain (who was more ready to spend money for mustering troops than giving it to the Electors) . . . This so increased the courage of those Electors favouring his cause, attracted others who were doubtful into their camp, and so frightened the Marquis of Brandenburg . . . with the result that finally coming to the act of election, Charles of Austria, king of Spain was elected as Emperor.

Source: Francesco Guicciardini, *History of Italy*, 1536, translated by S. Alexander, London, 1969

4.7 Charles V's aunt, Margaret of Burgundy, offers him advice

Margaret to Charles, 1519 (letter)

Sire, the matter of your election has long been discussed . . . we find that there are two ways by which you may arrange the election in your favour . . . the first is by cash . . . and the second, Sire, is by force. The French have plainly stated that they will win the Empire by way either of the affection in which Francis is held there or of money or of force. Since Francis wishes to employ force, he must be resisted by the same means. We believe, Sire, that you should order a large army to Roussillon and another to Navarre . . . by doing this, Sire, your reputation will increase throughout Germany which will advance your affairs and inspire fear in your enemies.

Source: M. Rady, *The Emperor Charles V*, London, 1988

4.8 Charles's abdication

From Charles's abdication speech, October 1555

Soon came the death of my grandfather Maximilian, in my nineteenth year, and although I was still young I sought and obtained the imperial dignity in his stead. I had no inordinate ambition to rule a multitude of kingdoms, but merely desired to secure the welfare and prosperity of Germany, my dear fatherland, and of my kingdoms, especially of my Belgian provinces; and to encourage and extend as far as in me lay Christian peace and harmony throughout the whole world.

Source: M. Fernandez Alvarez, *Charles V*, London, 1975

Document case-study questions

7 Explain 'Prelate Electors' in 4.6.

8 Comment on the attitude towards the election shown in 4.6 and 4.7, and contrast it with that of Document 4.8.

9 Is Guicciardini accurate in writing that Charles was 'more ready to spend money on mustering troops than giving it to the Electors'?

10 What does he estimate to have been the pope's motives for backing Francis, and are there others he does not mention?

11 How sound do you consider Margaret's advice in 4.7, and where had she gained her experience of practical politics?

12 In 4.8, Charles claims to have had 'no inordinate ambition' in seeking to become Emperor. Do you consider the reasons he gives are indeed the main ones?

5 Charles V: foreign policy

The men who influenced Charles

The roots of Charles V's foreign policy lie in the strong influence of his tutor and his governor as he was growing up. His tutor, Adrian of Utrecht, helped to form Charles into a deeply religious man and, when he became Holy Roman Emperor, he took his responsibility as lay head of Christendom and defender of the faith extremely seriously. Influenced also by Erasmus, his ultimate goal was universal peace throughout Christian Europe. In reality, he had to face the threat of the Lutherans within Germany, and almost continuous conflict with France. He also faced danger from Islam, with the Turks poised to attack in the east and across the Mediterranean.

Charles's governor, Chièvres, had also continually emphasised the importance of the Habsburg dynasty. The young prince grew up with a belief that it was his duty to preserve and, where possible, extend the influence of his family. Relatives were used as tools in the enterprise; few Habsburgs had a chance of marrying except to cement an alliance or gain a new sphere of influence for the dynasty. This ambition was lifted to new heights when Mercurino Gattinara, the Grand Chancellor, replaced Chièvres as chief adviser in 1521. Chièvres was a Netherlander, keen to keep on friendly terms with England and France. Gattinara came from Savoy and had a bolder and more international outlook. He wanted to make Italy the centre of Charles's interests, and to fill him with ambition to become a ruler with co-ordinated lands all over Europe, a true Empire. But the Emperor did not allow himself to be drawn into this plan to the extent Gattinara hoped. He realised that it was more realistic to allow each individual territory to retain its own institutions and distinctive rule.

The Emperor's problems

Fear of the Empire

Where Gattinara saw the huge extent of Charles's rule as an opportunity, many others saw it as a threat. The popes and the German princes shared the fear that an Emperor, who was also king of Spain, possessed enormous resources which could be used to force them to do his will. Francis I had an even stronger reason to share this fear; in every direction his country was bordered by lands under Charles's control. From Spain to the south, the Netherlands on the north-east, and down the whole eastern border from Germany through to north Italy, it must have seemed that Charles was in a position to squeeze France out of existence. Francis's response was to attack Charles wherever and whenever he could, making the Emperor's hope of lasting peace unachievable. If Charles won a victory, Francis made sure that it was soon followed by the creation of another anti-Imperial alliance. In his desperate search for aid against what he perceived as an ever-present threat, Francis even accepted help from the Turks and the German Protestant princes.

Shortage of money

If Charles's enemies had been fully aware of his financial situation, they might not have been so fearful. Throughout his reign, his foreign policy was hampered by his difficulties in raising money. Most of the cash for his wars came from Spain, the Netherlands and Naples. Germany contributed very little, as her Diets were able to resist Charles's demands. The States General of the Netherlands and the Castile *Cortes* were pressured into making the main contributions, although they grew increasingly reluctant. Wars became more costly as the years passed, with the demand for larger armies. All the time inflation eroded the value of the money flowing in. Bullion from the Americas helped, but only became a major source of income as the silver mines of Potosi began to be exploited in the 1540s. By then, Charles had become deeply indebted to a number of international bankers. Castile's Council of Finance was the main negotiator of loans, and by 1555 Charles had borrowed a staggering 29 million ducats. The interest on these loans was crippling, with each year's income largely mortgaged in advance to service the debt.

Charles needed the money to pay and equip his armies. There was no permanent Imperial army; forces had to be raised for each individual campaign. Spain provided well-trained troops, but the shortfall had to be made up with mercenaries, recruited mainly in Germany and Switzerland. Early in the reign, 20,000 to 30,000 soldiers had been sufficient, but by the end an army three times that size was needed. For the attack on Metz and the defence of Italy in 1552, Charles amassed a record 150,000 men.

War with Francis, 1521–29

It was fear of Charles's power, coupled with little awareness of the weakness underlying it, which led Francis to attack him in 1521. The two ambitious young men had already become competitors in the Imperial election. They also inherited a long-standing rivalry between their two families for control of Milan and Burgundy. Francis decided that a pre-emptive strike was better strategy than waiting for Charles to attack. The French had captured Milan from the Sforzas in the first campaign of Francis's reign in 1515; Charles's advisers showed him the need to oust the French from control of that part of northern Italy since it threatened the land route between Spain and the Netherlands.

Francis believed that Charles was too occupied with suppressing the *Comuneros* revolt to have troops free to withstand an attack, so he opened the war by sending his army to invade Navarre. He was too late: indeed some of the former rebels joined Charles's soldiers in repelling the foreigners. At the same time, Imperial troops advanced on Milan, where the French hastily withdrew. Five months later the two armies met at La Bicocca and, in spite of fresh reinforcements from home, the French were soundly defeated. Almost at once, Charles had yet another success in Italy, when his old tutor Adrian of Utrecht was elected as the new pope.

The reaction to Charles's success

It looked as if Charles was holding all the best cards. In a pattern that was to be frequently repeated, other countries hurried to ally with the victor. Henry VIII joined Charles and the pope in an offensive alliance with the object of invading France, and entertained Charles lavishly at Windsor to celebrate the treaty. Henry's daughter Mary was promised to Charles as his future bride, although she was only five years old.

An unexpected new recruit joined the anti-French side when the duke of Bourbon, one of the most powerful of Francis's nobility, turned traitor and put his forces at the allies' disposal (see page 83). This meant they were able to mount a triple attack on France in 1523: English troops would invade from the north, Imperial troops from the south, while Bourbon (who was still in France) would attack Francis's army from the rear as soon as it had crossed the Alps on its way to recapture Milan. However, the attacks were ill-co-ordinated and were soon called off as failures.

The Imperial victory at Pavia

The following year Francis led his army to Italy and recaptured Milan, but success was quickly followed by total disaster. Outside Pavia, Bourbon and the Imperial troops not only defeated the French army, but captured Francis. Charles hoped to make use of his power over his prisoner to force Francis to give up his claims in Italy and the Netherlands, and to promise to return Burgundy (part of which had been taken over by France after the death of Charles the Bold in 1477). When the French king failed to keep his promises once he was released, Charles could do nothing. Francis's two young sons were left as hostages in Madrid, sacrificed to their father's *realpolitik*.

The sack of Rome

Worse was to follow; Francis was now able to pose as the champion of Italy against Charles's over-mighty power. He quickly assembled an alliance (the League of Cognac) with the aim of driving the Habsburgs out of Italy for good. The Emperor turned to intrigue, stirring up the Italian enemies of the new pope, Clement VII, a member of the League. But this got out of hand when these enemies appealed to the duke of Bourbon and his Imperial troops for help against Clement. Acting without Charles's approval, he reached Rome in 1527 with his drunken German mercenaries, and was unable to stop them plundering the city.

In the years following this notorious sack of Rome, the balance tilted once more in favour of the French, as their troops succeeded in overrunning both Lombardy and Naples. Henry VIII was always ready to switch to the winner of the moment. Keen to get support in his campaign to end his marriage to Catherine of Aragon, Charles's aunt, he came back onto Francis's side. As long as the pope remained under Charles's control, he was exceedingly unlikely to grant a divorce. In a repetition of earlier events, the French found it impossible to hold on to distant lands in Italy. Finally in 1529, their army was defeated at the Battle of Landriano.

Temporary peace at Cambrai

Both sides were by now ready for peace, as neither could afford to continue fighting. This first phase of the conflict between Charles and Francis came to a close with the Peace of Cambrai in 1529. This was also called the Ladies' Peace, because it was negotiated by Louise (Francis's mother) for France and Margaret of Savoy (Charles V's aunt) for the Empire. The French surrendered their claim to Milan, Naples and Flanders, and promised to pay a large ransom for the two princes still held hostage in Madrid. Charles gave up his family's claim to the Burgundian lands held by Francis. Apart from this concession, he had gained what he wanted and remained in control of Italy. He hoped that, at last, the conflict with Francis was finished, and he could devote himself to Spain and Germany. To seal the peace, Francis was to marry Charles's sister, Eleanor of Portugal, and both men made empty promises to join in a crusade against the Turks.

The Turkish threat

Charles had spent most of the 1520s in Spain, directing the conflict with Francis from a distance. Meanwhile his brother Ferdinand had to cope with the spread of Lutheranism within Germany, and the very real menace of Turkish attack. Suleiman the Magnificent had been sultan of the Ottoman Turks since 1520. This most able and warlike leader, with vast resources of men and money, made no secret of his ambition to invade Christian Europe. In fact, one of Charles's reasons for seeking to become Emperor was that this would give him the means to lead a crusade against Suleiman.

In 1521, the Turks captured Belgrade (now capital of Serbia), and seemed poised to sweep up the Danube valley towards Budapest and Vienna. In fact Suleiman did not move again until 1526, by which time Francis had approached him as a possible ally. Now the Turkish army invaded Hungary, decisively crushing the army sent against them by Charles's brother-in-law, Louis, king of Bohemia and Hungary, at the Battle of Mohács in 1526. The young king and the bulk of his nobility were killed. Whatever horror overtook their country, Hungarians would always say 'More was lost on Mohács Field'. His widow, Mary, eventually replaced her aunt Margaret as regent of the Netherlands. Since she and Louis had no children, Ferdinand now became king, but he was faced with a rival claimant, John of Zapolya. Zapolya persuaded the Turks to back him, forcing Ferdinand to fight for his inheritance. Because he was in desperate need of help from the German princes, he dared not force them to join him in the suppression of Lutheranism.

Meanwhile Ferdinand had champions in Spain, the land where he had grown up. In 1527, the Castile *Cortes* urged Charles to send an army to Vienna to defend him against Turkish attack. But, for Charles, the war against Francis in Italy took priority, and the Spanish army, fitted out for Austria, found itself diverted to Rome. Instead of defending the eastern frontier of Christendom, they took part in the sack of Rome and the imprisonment of the pope. Charles's propaganda machine was hard put to present these extraordinary events in a good light. Fortunately, the expected attack on Vienna did not come at this point, and there was peace on the eastern frontier, as well as in Italy, by the time the Peace of Cambrai was signed.

The renewal of Imperial–French conflict

The peace did not last long. Francis was still anxious to regain Milan, and to attack and undermine Charles if the chance came. But this second phase of the Habsburg–Valois conflict was different from the first. There was very little fighting in Italy (Francis never recaptured Milan), and Francis now started to negotiate with Charles's enemies in earnest. He also strengthened his links with Pope Clement VII, when his eldest son, Henry, married the pope's niece, Catherine de' Medici, in 1533.

By now, Francis had also been on the receiving end of treachery. His Genoese ally, the powerful Admiral Andrea Doria, was bribed into changing sides, and became a valuable ally to Charles in the Mediterranean.

Conflict began again when Francis decided to retaliate against Charles's take-over of Milan when the last of the Sforzas died. He ordered his troops to capture Turin first but, when they journeyed on to attack Milan, they were unsuccessful. Nor did Charles's army succeed when, in a return move, it was sent to invade Provence. The two royal wives persuaded their husbands to make peace and actually come face to face before agreeing to the Truce of Nice in 1538. Once again, they promised to join in a crusade against the Turks.

War with Islam

The promise to join in a crusade was hypocrisy on Francis's part, as he was by now secretly negotiating with Suleiman as a possible ally. Charles had already taken a share in the defence of Christendom against Islam when he joined Ferdinand in strengthening Vienna against attack in 1532. He told his wife, 'I am determined that if the Turk comes in person . . . I shall face him myself.' He indeed led the large army himself and, although Suleiman's even larger forces came close to Vienna, the Turks did not risk fighting. Charles was justified in claiming that he had saved Vienna even though there was no actual battle.

Next, Charles turned his attention to the coast of North Africa, long the focus of Spanish forays against Islam. Suleiman's ally in the western Mediterranean was the ex-pirate, Barbarossa, based in Tunis. He had shown his strength by carrying out daring raids on the coast of Italy. In 1535, Charles sailed in person from Barcelona with a large fleet and army. He intended to capture Tunis, proclaiming before he left that this was a crusading expedition. In reality, the capture of Tunis had political advantages as well, giving the Spaniards control of Tunis and the Ottoman fleet based there. Charles had intended to follow up this victory with an attack on Algiers, but renewed war with France prevented this. When an expedition finally sailed for Algiers in 1541, a violent storm disrupted the enterprise. Much of the Spanish fleet was sunk or damaged, and rain dampened the gunpowder in the soldiers' arquebuses. The invaders had to go home unsuccessful. Charles's hopes were dashed that this would turn out to be a triumphant sequel to Tunis, and would help to reconcile the Spaniards to the huge sums they were pouring out for his wars elsewhere.

The final war with Francis, 1542–44

The conflict with France began again just one year later, in 1542. The alleged murder of two French secret agents, en route for Constantinople, gave Francis the pretext for declaring war. Both sides had, in fact, already been preparing for a future war. Charles had organised a double marriage between his son and daughter and the children of the king of Portugal. The Portuguese princess would come with a vast dowry, to add to the grants which Charles had already squeezed out of Castile and Aragon. Charles left his sixteen-year-old-son in charge as regent of Castile, and travelled north. He was accompanied by his best expert in international affairs, Nicholas Granvelle, soon to be assisted and then replaced by his son, Antoine. Meanwhile, Francis had been building links with some of the German Protestant princes and with Suleiman.

But dalliance with Muslims could also back-fire. Francis won himself universal condemnation throughout Christian Europe by allowing Toulon to be used as a base by Barbarossa. As a result, the Imperial Diet was happy to vote Charles enough money to pay for a formidable fighting force.

During two years of fighting, from 1542 to 1544, French attacks on Catalonia and the Netherlands were defeated. Imperial forces also invaded the Duchy of Cleves, Francis's German Protestant ally, and marched within a short distance of Paris. Henry VIII, taking advantage of what he saw as Francis's weakness, had already allied with Charles but, once again, proved unreliable. Instead of co-ordinating his attack with that of the Imperial forces, he concentrated on winning the French town of Boulogne for himself.

By 1544, shortage of money prevented Charles from finishing off the campaign with victory. Francis was also anxious to make peace, as the English continued to attack Boulogne. The terms of the resulting Peace of Crépy of 1544 repeated those of the 1538 Truce of Nice. It was intended as yet another final settlement, and Charles hoped that he could now concentrate his efforts in Germany. As

A portrait of the Emperor Charles V in 1548 by Titian (Tiziano Vecellio), c. 1488–1576.

usual, the peace was to be reinforced by a marriage, this time of a French prince with either the Emperor's daughter or his niece, with Milan or the Netherlands as a dowry. Perhaps it was fortunate that the young man died before a decision had been reached on this difficult choice.

Charles also hoped that Francis might assist him in persuading the pope to call a General Council and in dealing with the Lutherans. It was this lull in the wars against France that gave Charles the opportunity to concentrate his forces against the Schmalkaldic League and win victory at Mühlberg in 1547.

France and the German princes

Francis I died that same year, in 1547, and his son Henry II wanted time to settle in before contemplating a renewal of war. By the time he was ready to fight, Charles's high hopes of a final settlement of his German problems had turned to dust. The German Protestant princes had begun to plot against the Emperor. They could make use of growing nationalist feelings, as resentment increased against the Spanish garrisons stationed in many German towns. Once Francis was dead, Charles seems to have discounted the possibility of a link-up between the French and the German Protestants until it was too late. Henry II's ambassador signed a treaty of alliance with the League of Princes in 1551, which was ratified as the Treaty of Chambord the following year. In this, the French promised them a large sum of money in return for possession of three French-speaking towns under Imperial control, Metz, Toul and Verdun. All this time, Maurice of Saxony was playing a dangerous double game, secretly negotiating with the French and the Protestants, while publicly professing loyalty to Charles.

By 1552, Charles realised he was in real danger. He wrote to his son, Philip, in Spain, to ask for speedy help with money and troops, confessing his mistake in putting too much trust in Maurice of Saxony. Now he faced a nightmare coalition between his old enemies, the French, and the united German Protestant princes. Philip responded by raising all the cash he could, and by dispatching 5,000 Spanish soldiers to Germany. Although he was by now sick and exhausted, Charles was determined to defend the Empire and the Catholic faith to the best of his ability.

The final war began when one of the Protestant nobles of Brandenburg seized Donauwörth in south Germany. This triggered action by the other anti-Imperial allies, with the French occupying Metz and Maurice of Saxony and his confederates overrunning Franconia and Swabia. Charles panicked, seeing his troops on the run and his escape routes cut off, and fled to join Ferdinand in the Austrian Alps.

Yet the Emperor had not given up; he insisted that the 1552 Convention of Passau was only a temporary truce. Fresh troops and money arrived from Spain; Maurice of Saxony had abandoned his alliance with France and Charles sent out many feelers to try to win supporters among the different German princes and cities. But nothing came of them; he had effectively lost control of Germany. Yet he still hoped to oust the French, amassing a huge army to try to win back control of Metz. It was by now winter, and Metz held out successfully against him. Another of Charles's plans, to recapture Siena, was also a failure. All in all, the Emperor realised that the time had come for him to give up.

Charles's successes and failures

How far had Charles succeeded in realising those high aspirations with which his reign had started? The first aim, to defend Christendom against enemies both within and without, had not been a total failure. Obviously, the recognition of Lutheranism as a separate church and the consequent division of Germany was a tremendous defeat. Charles had, however, prevented Suleiman's forces from penetrating deep into Europe. Hungary had been lost to the Turks, apart from one small corner, but Austria had been saved.

Charles's hope that he could extend the power of the Habsburg dynasty had achieved some success. During his reign, he had made extensive use of members of his family as regents in his various lands, and as instruments in sealing alliances through marriages. His dream of handing on the whole Habsburg inheritance to his son, Philip, was not realised. At his abdication, he had divided it in two. Since, however, the combined Empire and Spain had proved too great a burden for one man, this split promised to strengthen the family, as long as the two wings remained close allies. This they did, until the Bourbons replaced the Habsburgs as kings of Spain a century and a half later. Charles's son Philip was left with the hope of furthering Habsburg dominance, by becoming ruler of Milan and the Netherlands, and by bringing England into the family's orbit as Mary Tudor's husband. The link with Portugal was successfully cemented by several marriages, including his own to Isabella of Portugal.

In spite of Erasmus' urgings, the aim of achieving peace was another which Charles could not attain. But, here, some of the blame can be laid on his persistent enemy, Francis I, who never rested from attacking the Emperor and creating coalitions against him. Whenever Charles won a victory, Francis was able to win allies by pointing out how great a threat was posed to all his neighbours by an over-mighty Emperor. In fact, that struggle, like the Lutheran problem, was only brought to an end after Charles's abdication. The French won the Battle of St Quentin in 1557, which was followed, two years later, by the final peace of the Habsburg–Valois wars, Cateau-Cambrésis.

Charles had been a slow youth, and was never quick in reaching a decision. Yet by the time he reached his prime, he had acquired a sound political judgement and won the respect of all those who dealt with him. Towards the end of his reign, however, the goal of peace had long been left behind. He became keen to pour ever greater resources into his wars, regardless of the damage this was doing to his subjects. One can point to numerous occasions where he failed to be alert to a danger, or made wrong estimations of human motive. The record of his reign, as a whole, however, shows a willingness not to spare himself in the service of his many lands, and wholehearted dedication to the ideals he held dear.

Peace and war

5.1 Erasmus on the conduct of a Christian prince

From Erasmus' manual, The education of a Christian prince, *1516. Erasmus, the humanist scholar, believed strongly that politicians should follow Christian principles. He dedicated this manual, written in 1516, to the young Prince Charles.*

Although a prince ought nowhere to be precipitate in his plans, there is no place for him to be more deliberate and circumspect than in going to war. Some evils come from one source and others from another, but from war comes the shipwreck of all that is good and from it the sea of all calamities pours out. Then, too, no other misfortune clings so steadfastly. War is sown from war; from the smallest comes the greatest; from one comes two . . . A good prince should never go to war at all unless, after trying every other means, he cannot possibly avoid it.

Source: *Collected works of Erasmus*, translated and annotated by N. M. Cheshire and M. J. Heath, Toronto, 1974

5.2 Charles's own thoughts on peace

From Charles's private memorandum for his own use, 1525

When I sat down to think out my position, I saw that the first thing at which I must aim and the best that God could send me, was peace. Peace is beautiful to talk of but difficult to have, for as everyone knows it cannot be had without the enemy's consent. I must therefore make great efforts – and that, too, is easier said than done. However much I scrape and save it is often difficult for me to find the necessary means. A successful war may help me. But I cannot support my army let alone increase it, if that should be necessary. Naples did not provide the money I hoped for . . . all sources of revenue here in Spain are daily tapped without result . . . The King of England does not help me as a true friend should . . . furthermore the armies are now very close to one another. A battle in which I shall be either wholly victorious or wholly defeated cannot be postponed for much longer . . . I can see no cause now why I should not do something great . . . I can think of no better way in which to improve my condition than by going myself to Italy.

Source: K. Brandi, *The Emperor Charles V*, London, 1939

5.3 The conflict between Francis and Charles

From Francesco Guicciardini's History of Italy, *Book 16, 1536*

Since at the battle fought in the park of Pavia, not only had the French army been shattered by the Imperial forces, but also the most Christian King taken prisoner . . . And after the imperial captains had won so memorable a victory with so little loss of blood, it is impossible to express how astonished were all the potentates of Italy . . . they were less reassured by what many divulged regarding the good intentions of the Emperor, and of his inclination towards peace, and not to usurp the states of others . . . than terrorised by considering the great danger that he . . . would turn his thoughts to making himself lord of all Italy . . . knowing how easy it is for every great prince to justify his enterprises with appearances that seem honest and reasonable.

Source: Francesco Guicciardini, *History of Italy*, translated by S. Alexander, London, 1969

Document case-study questions

1 Identify 'the most Christian King' in 5.3. Explain the word 'potentates' in 5.3.

2 Which factors does the Emperor identify as the main obstacles to the attainment of his objectives in 5.2?

3 What did Erasmus hope to achieve by dedicating his manual to Prince Charles in 1516? Suggest which recent wars are most likely to have influenced his opinions.

4 Bearing in mind the intentions expressed in 5.2, were the Italians justified in the fears they are shown to have felt after the Battle of Pavia in 5.3?

5 Making use of these documents, examine the main motives that governed Charles's foreign policy in the context of his career up to 1525.

The conflict with Islam

5.4 Turkish military success

Cardinal Ghinucci, writing from Venice, to Cardinal Wolsey in London, 23 September 1526 (letter)

Letters have arrived at Venice that the Turk had defeated the King [of Hungary] on 29 August, and that the King had not been found since. Letters from the Pope's nuncio confirm this, and say that the Turk . . . deceived the Hungarians by putting a few in an open place, and the rest concealed . . . In the battle, almost all the Hungarian foot deserted; they were partly Germans, partly Bohemians, partly Moravians . . . the Emperor's brother has gone with a small body of men to Vienna, which no one thinks can be defended . . . as it is not fortified and there are not enough troops.

Source: *Letters and papers foreign and domestic of the reign of Henry VIII*

5.5 Charles determines to defeat the Turks

Charles to his wife Isabella, April 1532 (letter)

I am determined that if the Turk comes in person, he will not do so unless he is at the head of a large army. Therefore I shall face him myself, and resist his attack with all the forces I can muster. With God's help – as I act in his cause – I will be helped and favoured, so that he may be served and our Holy Faith be exalted and strengthened.

Source: M. Fernandez Alvarez, *Charles V*, London, 1975

5.6 The capture of Tunis, July 1535

Charles's own account of the expedition

You know that with our Armada we came to Tunis to chase off Barbarossa and the other corsairs, enemies of our Holy Catholic Faith, and to restore King Muley Hassan to the throne, he having requested our help. We took by force the fortress of La Goletta. There the Turks lost everything . . . After occupying La Goletta we marched on Tunis . . . Barbarossa sortied from the town with his Turks to give battle. We attacked and defeated him entirely . . . Because the town's inhabitants did not appear to greet their restored sovereign as they should have done, and as he had a right to expect, we allowed the pillage of the place as punishment for their obstinacy.

Source: M. Rady, *The Emperor Charles V*, London, 1988

5.7 The attempt to capture Algiers, 1541

Charles explains his failure to take the town

After a few skirmishes, with everyone already suitably positioned to besiege the town and everything ready to batter it down, unexpectedly there was a great storm at sea, many vessels were lost and even those which lay at anchor were damaged. Everything possible was done to rally our strength to fight against the fury of the sea as much as against the attacks and assaults of the enemies on land.

Source: M. Fernandez Alvarez, *Charles V*, London, 1975

Document case-study questions

6 Explain the term 'nuncio' in 5.4 and 'corsairs' in 5.6.

7 Identify 'the Emperor's brother' in 5.4 and 'the Turk' in 5.5.

8 What does the description 'they were partly Germans, partly Bohemians, partly Moravians' reveal about the troops fighting for Hungary in this battle?

9 Point out the common factor explaining Charles's motivation in 5.5 and 5.6. Suggest two ways in which his conduct at Tunis in 5.6 indicates that he did not always keep to the high ideals he professed.

10 How far do these documents illustrate the range of the difficulties facing Charles in fulfilling his role of defender of Christendom against Islam?

6 Francis I: domestic policy

Francis's character

Francis I took the salamander as his emblem, the beast which, according to legend, could pass through fire unscathed. In the châteaux along the river Loire which Francis built or enlarged, the image of the salamander confronts the visitor again and again, often with its half-Latin, half-Italian motto, 'I feed upon the good and put out the evil'.

During his reign from 1515 to 1547, Francis made a serious attempt to live up to this motto. By the time he died, the king's position was more firmly entrenched, while his foreign policy had ensured France was respected as a major force. Those, moreover, who had tried to weaken the monarchy by power-seeking plots or by promoting heresy had been crushed. Under his patronage, the country had embraced the art and letters of the Italian Renaissance. France could more than hold her own with the other so-called new or Renaissance monarchies of the Empire, Spain and England.

Francis, like his contemporary Henry VIII in England, was a man of striking physical presence. Many portraits show him in profile, emphasising his long nose; all show his dark hair and eyes, and full-length pictures reveal his height and his girth. Again, like Henry VIII, he was capable of cruelty as well as a sensitive appreciation of beauty, and was also a shameless womaniser.

As the son of a distant cousin of the king, no one at his birth expected Francis to succeed to the throne. Yet a series of deaths in the French royal family made him heir presumptive by the time he was fourteen. He left his widowed mother's home, settled at court, and was betrothed to Claude, King Louis XII's daughter. France followed Salic law, by which only males could ever reign. By now, there was little chance that the ageing king would have a son, and when he died in January 1515, Francis became king.

France in 1515

The country he inherited was a smaller version of France as it is today, with considerable areas outside the king's jurisdiction: lands on the eastern border, a large tract north of Lyons, and the whole of Brittany. The country did not yet speak a common language, though the *langue d'oil* from which modern French derives was making rapid advances over the *langue d'oc* of the south. The

Francis I (1494–1547), panel by Jean Clouet (1485/90–1540).

population was around 15 million and growing fast. England's was less than a fifth of that figure. Farming was prospering, as fresh land was brought under cultivation to feed the extra mouths.

Paris and the other towns were all expanding because trade and industry shared in the growing prosperity. France's ports were sending goods to new markets as ships from Marseilles began to build up business in the eastern

Mediterranean, while the long-established wine trade brought ever greater riches to Bordeaux. New forges opened as the demand for metal rose; around Lyons the silk industry was expanding. Francis had inherited a country with huge potential.

Theories of royal power

At his coronation in Rheims Cathedral, Francis was anointed with holy oil, giving him the near-priestly powers long held by the kings of France. As well as being crowned, he was given the other royal insignia: the sword, symbolising military power, and the ring, sceptre and hand-of-justice (literally a piece of metal shaped like a forearm) symbolising judicial power.

These objects represented the medieval view of kingship, but Francis had become king when a rival concept was beginning to compete for acceptance. In the older theory, set out in 1515 by Claude de Seyssel in *La monarchie de France*, the king's power is restrained by religion, justice and a body of respected rights and practices which he calls 'la police'. (There is no exact equivalent in English: it can be translated as polity or police.) This means that the king's authority is not absolute; it can be checked by the church and by the courts. He occupies the top of a pyramid, in which many individuals and institutions, by agreement, share decision-making with the monarch.

The new theory, explained in 1518 by Guillaume Budé in *L'institution du prince*, gives greater power to the king. As God's representative on earth, he is owed the absolute obedience which is due to God himself. He does not share his authority, he merely grants privileges (which he can also take away); he is above the law (although he can choose to place himself within the framework of law and custom, to enhance the respect in which his subjects hold him: he does not wish to be a tyrant). This model, of a king with absolute power, appealed far more strongly to Francis than Seyssel's limited version of kingship.

The system of government

Francis had inherited a system of government that was based on the older model. It reflected the needs of a country that did not yet possess fixed frontiers, and within which some powerful nobles retained almost complete control over their own lands. This dated back to the days of feudalism, when kings granted estates to their greater subjects in return for military service. Many other individuals, and institutions such as town councils and local law courts, took for granted that they had a special relationship with the king. This was based on mutual need, in which each respected the other's rights and privileges.

To run this loosely organised country of 15 million people, with its assortment of semi-independent bodies and individuals, Francis had inherited a government machine that was creakingly unwieldy, slow and hard to direct. The royal court consisted of around 500 men, while the total of royal officials throughout the country was in the region of 5,000.

The King's Council
At the top, the King's Council consisted of a body of officials and powerful nobles, with an inner ring of the king's close friends and advisers, and sub-committees meeting from time to time to deal with specialised needs. The Chancellor was the head of the judiciary, the Constable commanded the armed forces, and these were the most powerful men in the kingdom after the monarch. A growing body of officials called *Maîtres des requêtes de l'hôtel* acted as links between central and local government, making sure that royal decrees were enforced.

Finance
Finance was in the hands of four *Trésoriers de finance*, collecting regular income such as the rents from the royal estates, and four *Généraux de finance*, who were responsible for collecting all the other government income. This came mainly from the taxes called the *gabelle* (a salt tax), *taille* (a poll tax) and *aides* (a general sales tax). These eight men formed the Finance Council, and had the task of outlining the national budget each year. Below them worked a bevy of tax officials and the locally elected citizens known as *élus*, who actually gathered the direct taxes in each area or *élection*. As inflation eroded the value of these sources of income, and huge debts accumulated as a result of Francis's wars, there was an urgent need for greater efficiency.

Justice
Justice was administered by local magistrates, with a tier of courts above them, one for each of the hundred districts, called *bailliages*, into which the country was divided. Above these, France also had seven regional courts called *Parlements*, mainly acting as appeal courts for cases from the *bailliages*. The Paris *Parlement* was responsible for the largest area by far, roughly two-thirds of the country. It had also won for itself the right to register royal edicts, and to issue regulations on all sorts of local issues such as the price of bread. Its growing political aspirations were to be a source of friction with the king during Francis's reign.

The States General and the Provincial Estates
Another potential source of friction existed in the shape of the States General and the Provincial Estates. The States General with its sub-divisions of Clergy, Nobles and Commons (the latter known in France as the Third Estate) had not been summoned since 1484. In theory, the king could call it at any time to consider a particular problem. The six major Provincial Estates, which met more frequently, were jealous of their privileges, and provided another possible conflict of interest with a king anxious to extend his authority. When the king consulted these bodies, the meetings tended to be taken up with the airing of members' grievances. Royal suggestions for change were almost always rejected for fear that they would infringe jealously guarded privileges. In addition, 11 provinces (later 16) had a governor, the king's representative in that area. Before modern communications, these men had the chance to gain a great deal of local power, although they also spent much time at court.

Francis's first war in 1515 and its impact at home

Francis could have started his reign by a thorough overhaul and modernisation of the machinery of government. Change would have been made easier by the fact that the two top posts, those of Chancellor and Constable were both vacant, so that Francis was able to appoint men of his own choice, Duprat and Bourbon. But military ventures were much more attractive to him than administrative reform, and Francis chose to start his reign by launching an ill-considered venture into Italy in pursuit of a distant claim to Milan (see page 81).

France's eastern borders were not firmly fixed, and Italy at that date was a tempting prey because of her wealth and her weakness. To a young man of Francis's upbringing and temperament, going to war was as natural and right as going off for a day's hunting. In September 1515, he won the Battle of Marignano and took control of Milan. The first impact of this campaign was on relations between the king and the church. Francis realised that if he were to keep a permanent foothold in Italy, he needed the support of the pope. Relations between France and the papacy had been soured many years earlier when an assembly of the French church, presided over by King Charles VII, had declared that a General Council of the church was superior in authority to the pope. This decision had been set out in the Pragmatic Sanction of Bourges, issued in 1438, and was bitterly resented by the papacy. Now, in his anxiety to gain the current pope, Leo X, as an ally, Francis was prepared to change his position on papal authority.

In return, Leo X agreed that Francis had the right to nominate candidates for all the main church posts in France. This replaced the old system by which, in theory, the cathedral clergy elected these candidates. In reality, French kings had exercised virtual control over the top church jobs for some time, but this position was made official by the Concordat of Bologna, agreed by Francis and Leo X in December 1515, and ratified the following year.

French clergy disliked a change that gave the pope a greater authority over the church, and also entrenched royal control. The movement for greater national rather than papal control over church affairs is known as Gallicanism. The *Parlement* of Paris supported it, and at first refused to register acceptance of the Concordat. Francis quickly grew impatient, issued threats, and so cowed the members into submission.

Meanwhile, the debts incurred by the Italian campaign were continuing to mount. By 1517, Francis was nearly 4 million livres in debt. To make matters worse, in 1519, he borrowed money to try to bribe the electors of the Holy Roman Emperor (without success). Two years later, the French lost control of Milan.

Financial reforms: the first wave

Drastic measures were clearly needed. The first and simplest course was to raise existing taxes. A second course was to make the financial machinery more efficient, so that more of the money collected reached the royal treasury and its expenditure was more closely monitored. Another course was to tap new sources of revenue. During the years of Francis's rule, all three methods were attempted.

The King's Council started with the first method, but tax collection was a slow business. Much money found its way into private pockets on its journey from the taxpayer to the royal treasury. Nevertheless, over the 32 years of Francis's reign, the income from the *taille* more than doubled in real terms, while income from the *gabelle* trebled. The yield from the *aides* also trebled.

To boost income quickly, Francis resorted to borrowing. Foreign bankers lent him a great deal; so did wealthy Frenchmen, and many towns were forced to make him loans. Selling crown lands brought in money that did not have to be repaid. Francis also hugely expanded the sale of official jobs and titles of nobility. The first and third of these methods had the drawback of creating a permanent need to pay interest; instant cash had been obtained at the cost of a long-term burden.

These measures all helped to ease the situation, but Francis and his councillors realised that the structure of the country's finances also needed to be changed to give better central control. A new war in 1521 had created a fresh crisis, and by 1523 the royal coffers were empty. Among other desperate measures, the king seized the treasure of Rheims Cathedral.

This time, a special inquiry, the *Commission de la tour carrée*, was set up to search out and punish dishonest officials, including the king's chief financial officer, Semblançay. But the king realised that a still more fundamental change was needed in order to reform the system that had given scope to these corrupt men. This started with the creation of a new post, the *Trésorier de l'épargne*, to deal with all the income outside the regular sources. Seeing the advantage of giving overall control to one man, Francis rapidly extended the *Trésorier*'s responsibilities, so that he received *all* the king's revenue. But the burden proved too great, and a year later the job was split in two: the *Trésorier de l'épargne* was put in charge of all the regular income from both rents and taxes, while the *Trésorier des parties casuelles* was given responsibility for every other type of income. (These two sources of income are often referred to as ordinary and extraordinary revenues.) The older posts of *Trésoriers* and *Généraux* were not abolished, but by-passed. From now on, since the *Trésorier de l'épargne* reported the king's week-by-week financial position to the King's Council, Francis had much greater awareness of his financial circumstances, and could exercise far stricter control of how the money was spent.

The 1523 Italian campaign and its consequences

Bourbon's treachery

The reforms were barely in place before fresh expenses were incurred by a new war, a pattern that was to occur time and again in Francis's reign. In 1523, the king decided to march to Italy again to try to recapture Milan. On his way there, he heard that his Constable, the duke of Bourbon, had turned traitor and sided with the enemy, Charles V. Fleeing to escape punishment did not save Bourbon from having his huge estates confiscated by the crown. This brought under Francis's control a part of the kingdom, the Bourbonnais, which had survived as a feudal anachronism, virtually an independent statelet.

Louise of Savoy's regency

The Italian campaign was a disaster and ended in Francis's captivity in Madrid for seven months. Louise of Savoy, Francis's mother, became regent during her son's long absence. Not only had she to run the country, but also to prepare for a possible invasion by Henry VIII and Charles V. She also had to agree conditions for Francis's release. Although she fulfilled her duties with care and skill, inevitably there were powerful men about who saw the chance to get their own way. Members of the Paris *Parlement* were among them; when Louise invited them to submit proposals to her, they took the chance to attack a whole range of Francis's policies. These included the lenient treatment of heretics.

She allowed *Parlement* to appoint four special commissioners to try suspected heretics, to define heresy in very broad terms, and to tighten censorship. This move put at risk several of the humanist scholars, who had been protected against accusations of heresy, until now, through Francis's personal intervention (see page 93). Only the news of the king's imminent return saved one of them, Louis de Berquin, from death by burning on this occasion.

Louise had won her son's release by agreeing to a humiliating treaty that involved handing over Burgundy and renouncing his claims in Italy and Artois. Francis had every intention of repudiating these terms as soon as he reached home, but he had to act cautiously because his two young sons had been left in Madrid as hostages.

Francis's re-assertion of authority

Once Francis was back in Paris, he quickly set about asserting his authority, and repairing what he saw as the damage done by his mother's pliability. Anne de Montmorency, from one of France's oldest and richest families, became head of the king's household and later Constable of France. Francis listened to his advice more and more, and his belief in a strong monarchy and orthodoxy in religion helped to reinforce the king's own inclinations. Francis also acquired a stunning new mistress, the duchesse d'Etampes. The king showed his ruthlessness by bringing to trial for a second time his chief financial officer, Semblançay, on charges of fraud, and this time he was found guilty. Probably Semblançay was no more dishonest than other royal officials, but he had lent large sums to the crown, and his death sentence released Francis from the need to repay him.

Francis believed he had a bone to pick with the *Parlement* of Paris, and summoned it to account for its actions during his captivity. The President was bold enough to tell him to his face that *Parlement* held its power from the people, not the king. Not surprisingly, Francis was enraged, and ordered his council to draw up an edict restricting the *Parlement*'s activities to its legal role, thus forbidding it to meddle in affairs of state. He had succeeded in nipping in the bud

Parlement's attempt to extend its authority into the area of politics, which would have diminished the power of the crown.

Francis also wanted to reverse the *Parlement*'s attacks on so-called heretics, who in his eyes were respectable and devout scholars. Humanist scholars, who had fled abroad for safety, were allowed to come home. But he failed to save one of them, Louis de Berquin. His trial for heresy was resumed; he was found guilty and, while Francis was away from Paris, was quickly burnt.

It was not until 1530 that the final terms of the peace treaty, by which Francis had been released from captivity in Madrid, were fulfilled. These involved the release, in return for a large cash ransom, of the two princes held as hostages in Spain and the arrival of Queen Eleanor of Portugal in France.

Further financial and judicial reforms

The year 1532 also saw a fresh innovation in the way the country's finances were organised. The *épargne* was created at the royal palace in Paris, the Louvre. All revenues were from now on to be paid into it (with the exception of the *parties casuelles*). In theory, this gave France a fixed, central treasury, but in reality officials were still able to by-pass it when they saw fit.

Yet each financial reform brought disappointing results, largely because new wars sent expenditure soaring, just as the royal coffers were beginning to refill. Francis was at war with the Empire again in 1536; the following year another campaign was planned, but had to be called off because there was no money left.

In 1539, the major Ordinance of Villers-Cotterêts was issued, with the aim of reforming the judicial system. Among its many clauses, the most famous are those ordering the registration of all baptisms, and the use of French instead of Latin in legal documents. It also abolished all confraternities (an early form of trade union), because a print workers' strike had angered the government. But printing was growing at a huge pace, and this clause was impossible to enforce.

After a brief period of friendship with Charles V, the underlying rivalry re-asserted itself and Francis declared war in 1542. The huge cost made it essential to squeeze fresh revenue out of the weary tax-payers, and to resort again to borrowing and to the sale of lands and offices. The package of measures, like that of the 1520s, started with administrative change. The old tax areas were split into smaller divisions and a new post, *Receveur général*, was created for each of them, with the duty of collecting all the revenue within that area.

A new tax was levied on walled towns and the *gabelle* was simplified. But simplification also involved removing exemptions, and the people of Guyenne, where much salt was produced, resisted the royal tax-collectors with armed force.

Francis went in person to La Rochelle to confront the rebels. They expected punishment, but were astonished when the king rewarded their apology with forgiveness. As a public relations exercise, it boosted the king's reputation, but in reality it was a sensible move at a time when Francis could ill spare troops to put down a real revolt. Another town, Lagny-sur-Marne, received harsh treatment two years later for similar defiance of royal orders.

Francis's final years

In his final years, Francis was an increasingly sick man. But this did not stop him dashing from one château to another in order to enjoy the best hunting, always accompanied by a coterie of beautiful ladies. Nor did it lead to any loosening of his hold on the country's affairs. His councillors reported to him both morning and evening, wherever he might be.

Since the death of the dauphin, Francis's two surviving sons had been on very bad terms. The king favoured the younger one, Charles, until his sudden death in 1545, and was unable to prevent factions growing up around each prince. These were further fuelled by the intrigues of the royal mistresses. Racked with pain from his many abscesses, Francis was downcast by the news of Henry VIII's death in January 1547, and only survived him by two months. On his death-bed, he is alleged to have warned his son not to allow others to rule him, and not to over-burden his subjects with taxes.

Following custom, the king's funeral took place at Notre Dame, and then the coffin was borne for burial to St Denis on the outskirts of Paris. Once he was in control, the new king, Henry II, set about a great moral cleansing of the court, and the replacement of his father's most powerful advisers.

Henry inherited a country more unified than in 1515, with the crown's control of the administrative and financial machinery increased, but with an empty treasury. Francis's reputation received an undeserved and short-lived boost after his death, when the story went round that he had left large quantities of cash. In reality, this sum had been loaned by the bankers of Lyons, and was almost as large as the entire royal income for the year. Francis had left a huge debt, not a huge surplus, and Henry II had the task of repaying it.

Yet he also left a far more admirable legacy. Many of the palaces that he built and the paintings and sculpture that he commissioned from Italy's finest artists are still there for us to enjoy. Francis backed Cartier's exploration of Canada; he built the port of Le Havre to foster overseas trade and encouraged home industry by curbing imports. These achievements, not his wars or his mistresses, are what he deserves to be remembered for.

Document case studies

Francis I's domestic policy

6.1 Claude de Seyssel's view of the monarchy

From Claude de Seyssel's The monarchy of France, *1515. Claude de Seyssel had served Louis XII as councillor and presented this book as a manual to the new king. He commends monarchy as the best form of government, believing that the French kings' strength came from their commitment to the rule of law, their respect for their subjects' rights and privileges, and their devotion to the Christian faith.*

Of these bridles by which the absolute power of the king of France is regulated I deem that there are three main ones. The first is religion, the second justice, the third polity . . .

As to the first it is certain that the people of France have always been and still are devout and religious above all other people and nations . . . so it is essential that whoever is king here make known to the people by example and by present and overt demonstration that he is a zealous observant of the Christian faith and wishes to maintain and augment it to the best of his ability . . . If the king lives in accordance with the Christian religion and law (at least in appearance) he can scarcely act tyrannically . . .

The second bridle is justice, which beyond any doubt is in greater authority in France than in any other country of the world that we know of, especially on account of the Parlements, which were instituted chiefly to bridle the absolute power that the kings might want to use . . .

The third bridle is that of polity, that is to say, the many ordinances, made by the kings of France themselves and afterwards confirmed and approved from time to time, which tend to the conservation of the realm in general and in detail. These have been kept for such a long time that the princes never undertake to derogate from them; and if they wanted to do so, their commands would not be obeyed.

Source: J. H. Shennan, *Government and society in France, 1461–1661*, London, 1969

6.2 Guillaume Budé on the importance of royal authority

From Guillaume Budé's L'institution du prince, *1518. Budé was a humanist scholar who believed that the king's right to absolute power made it essential that he received the right education.*

Kings are subject to neither laws nor ordinances if they do not seem good to them.

Source: J. W. Allen, *Political thought in the sixteenth century*, London, 1928

6.3 The powers of *Parlement*

Edict defining the Parlement's powers, July 1527

To Messieurs their presidents and councillors of his court of *Parlement* . . .

The king forbids you to meddle in any way in affairs of state or in anything other than justice and commands that each year you shall obtain letters confirming your delegated authority, as was done formerly . . .

He forbids you to judge all matters archiepiscopal, episcopal and abbatial, and declares null and void any attempt by you to contravene this ban. He also cancels all the limitations imposed by you on the power and regency of his mother. He has revoked and annulled all that you have attempted in dealing with cases on appeal, appointments, etc. The king confirms all that was done and commanded by the regent . . . He orders that all that has been registered by the *Parlement* against her authority shall be sent to him for cancellation.

The king forbids the court to apply in future any limitation, modification or restriction to his ordinances, edicts and charters . . .

The king declares that you have no jurisdiction or power over the chancellor of France. This belongs to the king alone and no one else. Consequently he has cancelled all your acts directed against the chancellor . . .

The king wishes the present edict to be registered by his Conseil Étroit, Grand Conseil, and *Parlement*.

R. J. Knecht, *French Renaissance monarchy*, London, 1984

Document case-study questions

1 Explain in your own words Seyssel's third check on the king's absolute power in 6.1.

2 What is the significance of the term 'delegated authority' in 6.3?

3 In Seyssel's view, how does the king's religion prevent him from ruling as a tyrant?

4 Explain why Francis believed he had to confirm the regent's authority at this time.

5 Compare the king's power in relation to ordinances, as shown in the three documents.

6 Seyssel uses the term 'absolute power' in 6.1. How would you define this, and in the light of 6.3, how far would you consider that Francis heeded Budé's advice rather than Seyssel's?

Francis I's character

6.4 Francis to his mother, Louise of Savoy

Francis to Louise of Savoy on his way to fight in Italy in 1515 (letter)

Madame, we are in the strangest country that any man of this company has ever seen. But tomorrow I hope to be in the plain of Piedmont with the troops I command, which will please us all as it is troublesome wearing armour in these mountains because most of the time we have to go on foot and lead our horses by bridle. Those who do not see it will not believe that anyone could bring over horsemen and heavy artillery in the way we are doing. Certainly, Madame, it has not been without difficulty; if I had not come, our heavy guns would have stayed behind.

Source: D. Seward, *Prince of the Renaissance*, London, 1973

6.5 Francis to his mother, Louise of Savoy

Francis to his mother after he had been captured at Pavia, 1525 (letter)

Madam. To let you know the extent of my misfortune, nothing remains to me but my honour and my life which are safe. And so that news of me may be of some small comfort to you, I have begged to be allowed to write this letter, which favour has been given to me freely. I beg you not to lose heart but to employ your usual good sense, for I have confidence that in the end my God will not desert me. I commend unto you my little children, who are also yours, and beg you to hasten the bearer of this on his road to and from Spain.

Source: D. Seward, *Prince of the Renaissance*, London, 1973

6.6 The court

Rabelais' description of dress worn at the fictitious Abbey of Thélème (based on his own observations at Francis's court)

The men were apparelled after their fashion . . . their doublet was of cloth of gold . . . embroidered and suitably trimmed up in perfection . . . their caps or bonnets were of black velvet, adorned with jewels and buttons of gold . . . their gowns were every whit as costly as those of the ladies . . . their beads, rings, bracelets, collars and neck-chains were all of precious stones.

Source: *The histories of Gargantua and Pantagruel*, translated by J. M. Cohen, London, 1955

6.7 Francis's fondness for women

From the memoirs of Gaspard de Saulx de Tavannes, Marshal of France and a member of Francis's court

Alexander the Great saw women when he had no business . . . Francis attended to business when he had no more women . . . everywhere the ladies had too much power.

Source: D. Seward, *Prince of the Renaissance*, London, 1973

6.8 The view of the Venetian ambassador

The Venetian ambassador's description of Francis, 1546

His appearance is quite regal, so that even without having his face or his portrait, simply by looking at him, one says immediately 'this is the king'. His movements are so noble and majestic that no prince can equal him. His character is sturdy, in spite of the excessive fatigues which he has always endured and still endures in so many expeditions and journeys. Very few men could have supported such adversities . . . He eats and drinks a great deal; sleeps even better, and, what is more, he thinks only of leading a gay life. He is careful about his dress, which is full of braids and trimmings, rich in precious stones and ornaments; even his doublets are woven with gold thread . . . if the king endures bodily fatigues unflinchingly, he finds mental preoccupations more difficult to bear and hands them over almost entirely to the cardinal of Tournon and the admiral. He takes no decisions and gives no reply without first listening to their advice; in all things he follows their counsel . . . But in all the great matters of state, matters of peace and war, His Majesty, who is submissive in everything else, insists on his will being obeyed . . . This prince has a sound judgement and wide learning; there is no object, study or art on which he cannot argue pertinently or judge with as much assurance as a specialist. His knowledge is not confined simply to the art of war . . . he understands not only all that concerns naval warfare but is also very experienced in hunting, painting, literature, languages and the bodily exercises appropriate to a good knight. Truly, when one sees that in spite of his knowledge and fine speeches, all his martial exploits have failed, one says that all his wisdom is on his lips, not in his mind. But I believe that the adversities of this prince are due to the lack of men able to carry out well his designs.

Source R. J. Knecht, *French Renaissance monarchy*, London, 1984

Document case-study questions

7 What is meant by 'martial exploits' in 6.8?

8 Identify Louise of Savoy in 6.5 and explain why Francis begs her to 'hasten the bearer . . . on his road to and from Spain'.

9 Contrast the tone and circumstances 6.5 and 6.6, and show what they reveal about Francis's character.

10 Explain the assertion of the writer of 6.7 that 'everywhere the ladies had too much power'. Is it borne out by 6.8?

11 How far is the description of Francis in 6.8 corroborated by the other documents, and by your own knowledge of him?

7 Francis I: foreign policy

Francis's objectives

The prime goal of Francis's foreign policy was the assertion of his own and his country's power through successful campaigns, with Italy, and especially Milan, as his main target. His second aim was the protection of France and new lands he acquired. As previously shown, this policy led him into frequent wars. These placed a great strain on France's finances, again and again using up the savings made in years of careful management.

Yet, at first sight, his foreign policy appears to consist of a chaotic sequence of mainly fruitless campaigns and shifting alliances, with no real achievement at the end. One way to try to explain Francis's actions, is to compare them to a game of chess, where the aim is to capture an opponent's strongest pieces, but at the same time to protect one's own position. Francis was, by nature, an aggressive campaigner. For much of his reign, his main aim was to win control of parts of Italy. But from 1519 onwards, his policy was dominated by fear of the Holy Roman Empire, leading him to spend much energy on defensive moves. In both his offensive and defensive actions, he had to consider the advantages of seeking allies. Part of the complexity of Francis's foreign policy lies in the frequency with which this year's ally becomes next year's enemy.

Francis's Italian ambitions

The expeditions of Charles VIII and Louis XII

Francis was also influenced by the successes and failures of his predecessors. Both the previous kings, Charles VIII and Louis XII, had led armies into Italy in pursuit of key territories (Naples and Milan). They claimed these were theirs by right of inheritance through long-dead ancestors. These struggles are aptly named the Habsburg–Valois Wars, since they furthered the interests of the rival dynasties of France and the Holy Roman Empire rather than those of the countries themselves. Italy was not only conveniently next door, but in the late-fifteenth century was extremely wealthy. Capture of any of the leading Italian cities brought booty as well as prestige. At the same time, the fact that Italy was divided between many different rulers made it an easy prey for a determined attacker.

Both Charles and Louis had captured their Italian targets relatively easily, but had found the prizes impossible to hold in the long term. There was high expectation, at the beginning of his reign, that Francis would try to recapture Milan, and possibly Naples, and avenge the recent French failures. In fact, Italy was beginning to be a less easy target. The medieval walls that had crumbled so quickly under the onslaught of the new iron cannonballs of the late-fifteenth century were being replaced by far stronger fortifications. Italian rulers were growing wise to their need to make alliances for mutual defence, and also to the advantages of siding with the winner in disputes beyond Italy.

The 1515 attack on Milan

Neither of these dangers was apparent at the start of Francis's reign. As soon as he was crowned, he began to plan an attack on Milan, at that time under Maximilian Sforza's rule. It was only two years since Louis XII had mounted a disastrous attempt to regain Milan and Naples; yet the French forces were already keen for a new attempt. They believed they had a good chance of success under a vigorous young king, who regarded fighting as a nobleman's natural occupation.

Like a good chess player, Francis first covered his rear, by persuading his neighbours to remain neutral while he was away. Both Charles of Burgundy, the ruler of the Low Countries, and Henry VIII of England were willing to comply at this stage. He also sought allies among the rulers of other parts of Italy. Venice and Genoa offered to help in return for concessions, but the pope, the king of Aragon, who ruled Naples, and the Emperor Maximilian all agreed to ally with the duke of Milan in defence of Italy against a French attack.

Undeterred by this partial setback, Francis prepared his forces for the campaign. He already had the largest standing army and the strongest artillery in Europe. The French army's best troops were its cavalry, so Francis recruited 23,000 German mercenaries to build up his infantry. At this time, Swiss mercenaries were the best foot soldiers in Europe but, on this occasion, they had been recruited by the enemy. Finally, Francis arranged for his mother to be in charge of the kingdom while he was away.

In late July 1515, he joined his army in south-east France, ready to cross the Alps by a little-known route. The French marched rapidly eastwards towards Milan, but at the same time Francis was negotiating with Sforza and the Swiss to see if he could win the city without a fight.

However, many of the Swiss mercenaries waiting to defend Milan were distrustful at news of these negotiations, which they saw as a potential sell-out by their masters. They decided to make a surprise attack on the French army, by now encamped at Marignano. After early Swiss success, Francis regrouped his forces, who were given fresh heart by the arrival of reinforcements from Venice. Unwilling to fight on, the Swiss retreated to Milan and Sforza realised he had no hope of defending his city. He agreed to hand it over to Francis and to go into exile in France.

Francis had not only won Milan, but found that he was also able to buy the support of the Swiss cantons and their crack troops. Yet he realised that he still had many enemies in Italy. Believing that the pope was the prime mover in constructing anti-French alliances, he made it his business to go straight from

Milan to Bologna to meet Pope Leo X, who was a member of the great Medici family of Florence.

Early-sixteenth-century popes put political considerations first, and Leo X was keen to gain Francis's support for Florence in any future war. He and Francis negotiated the Concordat of Bologna, which they both hoped would seal the close co-operation of France and Rome after many years of hostility. Popes had another reason for seeking the support of secular rulers: even at this late date, they still hoped to lead a crusade of Christian armies to recapture Constantinople from the Turks. This pipe-dream was long used as the cement for otherwise shaky alliances of rival rulers, with diminishing effect.

The Imperial threat: war with Charles

Up to this point, everything had gone according to plan for Francis. But, in 1516, the accession of Charles of Burgundy, the future Emperor, to the Spanish throne was the first step in a major shift in the balance of power in Europe. For the moment, Charles was anxious for French friendship, since he still had to establish his control in Spain. He signed the Treaty of Noyon with Francis; another potential enemy, Henry VIII, took this as a cue and decided to rein in his aggressive intentions for the time being.

The impact of the Imperial election

The death of Charles's grandfather, the Emperor Maximilian, in 1519 led to the second step in the shift of power in Europe. If Charles was elected as Holy Roman Emperor, he would rule an enormous swathe of territory encompassing the Low Countries, Spain, and present-day Germany and Austria. This would effectively encircle France and, perhaps, menace her very existence.

Charles's succession as Emperor was not a foregone conclusion. Both Francis and Henry VIII were keen to put themselves forward as candidates in the trad-itional election for this most prestigious crown. Neither realised that the German Electors who made encouraging noises to them were merely pushing up the price of their votes. In the event, the candidate able to pay the largest bribes was the winner, and Charles's access to German bank loans put him in that position.

Charles's victory led Henry VIII to seek Francis as an ally against this threateningly mighty new ruler. He believed England's advantage lay in a more even balance of power in Europe. Henry was to change sides several times during Charles's reign as he saw first the Empire, and then France as the greater threat. For the moment, Henry and Francis swore friendship at the 1520 feat of arms, the famous Field of the Cloth of Gold, that took place on English territory, near Ardres, in present-day France. In fact, Henry hedged his bets by welcoming Charles on a brief visit to England soon after.

The loss of Milan

Francis's declarations of friendship to both Charles and Henry were short-lived. He had decided that his only hope of survival in the face of a potential enemy with such strength was to foment trouble for the Holy Roman Emperor whenever and wherever possible. His first attempt, which involved backing an attack on Luxemburg, ended in failure. Soon after, both England and the pope had changed sides to support the Empire. Worse still, the French commander of Milan had made himself so unpopular with its citizens that they welcomed the Imperial forces when they attacked the city in 1521. Within a short time, the French had been driven out of Italy. An attempt to recapture the lost lands the following year ended in defeat at the Battle of La Bicocca, when the Swiss deserted their French masters who were too short of cash to pay them.

Anti-French alliances

By 1523, Henry and Charles were planning a joint invasion of France, taking advantage of her troubles. England still owned Calais, but the Imperial–English army soon had to abandon its attack on Picardy because it was running short of supplies. With one danger over for the moment, Francis embarked on a fresh Italian campaign to try to recapture Milan. But foreign enemies were not Francis's only problem; at this crucial moment, his Constable (the duke of Bourbon) turned traitor, angered by Francis's attempt to seize lands owned by Bourbon's late wife.

Francis was actually on his way to Italy when the news reached him. He broke his journey to visit Bourbon at home to try to win him back. When that failed, he decided to stay in France to quell the rebellion that he suspected Bourbon was plotting. In addition, he had news that Charles and Henry were about to invade France as Bourbon's allies. In the event, both those attacks failed, and Bourbon by then had fled, first to Franche-Comté, and then to Italy. Eventually he put himself and his troops at the Emperor's disposal.

Defeat at Pavia

In the summer of 1524, Bourbon, in his absence, was tried and found guilty of treason. Francis then felt ready to continue the long-delayed Italian expedition. This time there was no easy victory. The French army suffered a series of minor defeats and Bourbon, encouraged by the Emperor, invaded Provence. Once more, Francis had to deal with the danger closer to home before he could risk leaving the country. By the time Bourbon had been forced to retreat, it was late autumn. Francis took a great risk in attacking so late in the year. At that time, armies never fought in winter because they had no means of transport through mud and snow. The French besieged Pavia. After nearly four months encamped outside the city walls, Francis and his army were caught by a surprise enemy attack. Within a few hours they had suffered a crushing defeat, and Francis was taken prisoner. He was moved by slow stages to Madrid, where he remained in captivity until early in 1526. Although the royal prisoner was confined in a palace, not a cell, a diplomat who saw Francis there reported that 'it was a pitiable sight'.

Negotiations for Francis's release

Francis's mother, Louise of Savoy, was now presented with very heavy demands by Charles V. Francis was to give up Burgundy and land near Calais, pardon Bourbon, and set up a new independent kingdom for him in Provence. To seal the treaty, as was customary, there would be a wedding, this time between the dauphin and Charles's niece Mary. When Francis was told of these terms, he expressed his determination to hold on to Burgundy at all costs.

Meanwhile, Louise realised that it would strengthen France's bargaining position if the Emperor lost England as an ally. With much skill, she sent her envoys to London to conclude peace with Henry VIII, and to gain his support in persuading Charles to soften his demands. She also put out feelers for a new anti-Imperial alliance of Italian rulers who felt threatened by Charles.

Charles remained adamant that Francis must give up Burgundy, refusing to accept the offer of a vast ransom instead. Desperate to get free, Francis made promises that he never intended to keep. He agreed to the Treaty of Madrid, by which he was to surrender Burgundy and his claims in Italy and re-instate Bourbon. On his way home from Spain, Francis met the Emperor's sister, Eleanor of Portugal, who was to be his second wife as part of the treaty terms. He also witnessed the handing over of his two young sons, to become hostages in Spain till the terms of the treaty were fulfilled.

Francis waited before repudiating his promise to hand over Burgundy to Charles. To strengthen his position, he persuaded the Burgundian Estates to declare their determination to remain part of France. It was providential that the Emperor was by now too involved with problems elsewhere and too short of money to contemplate seizing Burgundy by force.

League of Cognac and renewal of war

Charles rejected Francis's offer of cash instead of Burgundy, and the young princes remained hostages in Spain. The king needed to strengthen his hand in bargaining with Charles without risking war. The obvious course was to make alliances with Charles's current enemies, the ploy that Francis was to use so often. First he signed a new agreement with Henry VIII, then he joined the League of Cognac, an alliance of the pope, Venice, Florence and the duke of Milan aimed at expelling the Imperial troops from Italy.

Francis regarded the League as a means to his own private end, his sons' release, but for the other members it was the first move in a war against Charles. They wanted to take advantage of the Emperor's vulnerability at this point, with Lutheranism gaining ground in Germany. But Charles was stronger than they had reckoned. Their hopes were not only unrealised, but to make matters far worse, Imperial troops under Bourbon's control sacked Rome in 1527 and took the pope prisoner.

This was the event which was to have such serious repercussions in England since the pope was now controlled by Catherine of Aragon's nephew, Charles V, and would refuse Henry a divorce. It also gave England fresh reason to be friendly towards France, as Charles's enemy.

Quickly Francis persuaded Henry to join him in making war on Charles, with the declared objective of rescuing the pope. French troops had already invaded Lombardy; now they were sent on south to besiege Naples, and the following year another French army tried to win Genoa. But the old story was repeated: after early success, the French troops were driven out. Their collapse convinced the pope that he would be wiser to back the stronger ruler, the Holy Roman Emperor, rather than Francis.

The Peace of Cambrai

With nothing achieved, by 1529 all the rulers concerned were ready to make a peace that was meant to last. In the resulting Peace of Cambrai, Charles agreed to free Francis's sons and to accept a huge sum in gold in place of Burgundy. Francis gave up his claims to cities in Italy and on France's northern borders. To seal the Treaty, Francis's marriage to Eleanor would at last take place.

Charles hoped that this peace was a final settlement of his wars with Francis, freeing him to concentrate on the many problems facing him within his own territories. But Francis saw it differently, as a pause to recover strength and consolidate his position in France after his absence. When ready, he intended to resume his attacks on Charles, since he believed the Emperor was a continuing threat. Nor had he abandoned his Italian ambitions; Charles was too strong to be attacked on his own territory, but Italy still seemed to provide a theatre where there was room to fight him with a chance of success.

Negotiations with the Emperor's enemies

Charles's hopes of a lasting peace were soon shattered, as Francis started to make trouble for him on the principle that 'my enemy's enemy is my friend'. The Emperor's uneasy relationship with the German princes had become far worse with the advent of Protestantism. When a group of them formed the Schmalkaldic League, to defend their interests against Charles, and appealed for Francis's help, he could not resist this chance to undermine Charles's position at home.

Meanwhile, Henry VIII was anxious for Francis's support in his struggle to gain the pope's agreement to his divorce. This gave Francis the opening for a bargain: he asked Henry to share the cost of subsidising the German princes, and, in return, he promised to put pressure on the pope. Francis did meet the pope in 1533, but all he gained from it was an agreement that the pope's niece, Catherine de' Medici, would marry Francis's second son, Henry.

Francis also started negotiating with a Muslim pirate known as Barbarossa, who was about to attack Tunis (held at that time by an ally of the Emperor). This may seem an extraordinary move for a Christian ruler who was also prepared to talk about a possible crusade against Islam. In fact, Francis had already sent an envoy to Constantinople in an unsuccessful attempt to persuade the sultan to launch an attack on the Empire through Italy. Such negotiations show the lengths to which Francis was prepared to go in order to stir up trouble for Charles.

Yet, in the mid-1530s, Charles still appeared to be in the ascendant. Francis had lost the trust of the German Lutheran princes by his harsh treatment of those of his own subjects who were Protestants. In 1535, Charles successfully captured Tunis and went on to Sicily at the start of a victorious progress through Italy.

The re-opening of the war against Charles

Francis was not yet ready to attack Charles openly. However, the death of Francesco Sforza, the duke of Milan since 1525, spurred him on to claim the duchy on behalf of his second son, Henry. When Charles objected, Francis decided to give himself a bargaining counter by invading Savoy, ruled by Charles's ally and brother-in-law. In reply, Charles ordered his troops first into Piedmont and then straight on into Provence. At the same time, he ordered an invasion of northern France to force Francis to divide his troops. This was in high summer, and not for the first time a campaign had to be abandoned because the army could not cope with an outbreak of disease. This had been made much worse by rotting food, polluted water and primitive camp sanitation. Meanwhile, Francis's commander, Montmorency, had not only been preparing to defend Provence after a series of strategic retreats, but had built his camp with such care that his troops stayed healthy.

That summer of 1536 brought Francis bad news as well as good; his eldest son died suddenly, so the second son, Henry, now became dauphin. Montmorency was rewarded with the post of Constable which had been vacant since Bourbon's defection. Both sides were, by then, further exhausted by minor campaigns in northern France and in Piedmont, and were also running short of money. They were ready to call a halt, but it was only a pause; no agreement could be reached on the future of Milan.

Montmorency as an influence for peace

For the next two years, from 1538 to 1540, Montmorency had a strong influence on Francis. He believed that France had more to gain from peace than war with the Empire, and persuaded his master that, in the long run, he could even win Milan by this new policy. The pope had just formed a new Holy League to fight the Turks, enrolling the Emperor and hoping for French support. This provided an opportunity to bring Charles and Francis together in Nice. Although Francis petulantly refused to meet Charles personally, the pope was able to get both rulers to agree to a long truce. Eventually Queen Eleanor, Francis's wife and Charles's sister, managed to organise a face-to-face meeting at Aigues-Mortes, further west along the coast.

Friendly relations continued throughout 1539, with Francis inviting Charles to travel through France on his way from Spain to Flanders to quell a revolt. Charles was given a sumptuous reception, but the reward of Milan, which Francis hoped to reap from this generosity was not offered. Instead, Charles proposed various marriages, including that of his daughter Mary to Francis's second son, Charles, with the pair eventually inheriting the Netherlands. For Francis, the Netherlands were no substitute for Milan, and before long the negotiations collapsed.

Montmorency's fall and the return of war

Montmorency's ascendancy made him many enemies at court. Francis's mistress, the duchesse d'Etampes, was one of the leaders, and she now declared that the Constable was 'A great scoundrel, for he has deceived the king by saying that the Emperor would give him Milan at once when he knew the opposite was true'. When news came that the Emperor had given Milan to his own son, Philip, Montmorency's influence was over and the king turned once again towards war. Francis began, in his usual way, by seeking allies against Charles: the Protestant duke of Cleves (brother of Henry VIII's brief bride), the Schmalkaldic League and the sultan of Turkey. His suspicions that Charles, too, was planning war were fuelled by the murder of two French envoys and the Emperor's arrival in Algiers.

Charles's expedition to North Africa failed, but so did Francis's attempts to gain the German princes and the English as firm allies before launching an attack. In July 1542, news reached Paris that the French envoy at Constantinople had persuaded the sultan to pledge huge support to Francis in men and money, and this gave the king the confidence to declare war on Charles. This was followed by French attacks on Luxemburg on her northern border and Perpignan in the south, of which only the Luxemburg one was successful.

By now, Henry VIII had decided it was time that England took advantage of the new war, by making an alliance with the Empire against France. At once, an English force was dispatched towards Boulogne and, later that summer, the Emperor launched an attack on Cleves. Neither side, however, had made any real conquests before winter closed the campaigning season.

Turkish Toulon

Startling, if not shocking events were, meanwhile, unfolding in the south of France. The sultan had kept his promise to provide Francis with naval and military help, and his fleet succeeded in bombarding and capturing Nice (at that time, part of Savoy). When the Turks demanded a base to refit their ships, the king handed them Toulon, ordering the inhabitants to evacuate the port. For eight months, 30,000 Turks made a base here on the coast of Provence, a Muslim enclave in Christian France, complete with a mosque and a slave market.

Francis won himself universal condemnation by showing the lengths to which he would go in order to win allies. When they finally left France, the Turks added to the king's embarrassment by raiding the coast of Italy for slaves on their voyage home. The whole episode had gained Francis nothing.

The Anglo–Imperial attack on France

Later in 1543, the pope sent his envoys to Francis and Charles to try to bring peace, but by now the Emperor was determined to invade France in conjunction with his ally, England. One army was to come from the north, the other from the east, and they hoped to march ahead, meet in Paris and force Francis to accept their terms. Charles believed this could be his final war with France, and he publicly accused Francis of being a tyrant and friend of Muslims who deserved destruction.

Although Henry and Charles confidently accompanied their troops in person, the French defence was stronger than expected. Even so, there was a time of panic in Paris, and Francis set to work to divide his enemies by diplomatic means. Henry VIII was unresponsive to peace feelers, since he had set his heart on capturing Boulogne (which he gained that autumn). But, as so often before, Charles was soon anxious to make peace and return to Germany because he had received news of fresh religious troubles at home. He signed the Peace of Crépy with Francis, by which the French king's younger son, Charles, was to marry the Emperor's daughter or niece. As a dowry, the prince would receive either the Low Countries and Franche-Comté or Milan.

The prince's death the following year rendered these arrangements void, but already France's allies, England and Turkey, felt they had been betrayed, as they were willing to go on fighting. Henry VIII continued to resist Francis's peace proposals, and to put pressure on him the French king sent troops to Scotland and despatched his fleet to attack the south coast of England. While she was helping to defend the Solent, the warship *Mary Rose* keeled over and sank to the bottom, there to rest for 450 years.

The final peace

Neither king could win. Money was running short, and eventually peace terms were worked out between them. By the Peace of Ardres, in June 1545, Henry agreed to hand back Boulogne to Francis in return for the payment of two million *écus*. Yet, again, Francis's ambition had resulted in the need for a huge amount of cash, to be raised with great difficulty from an already exhausted country.

In the last months of his reign, Francis was once again using the old ploy of negotiating with the Emperor's enemies. By now, the Schmalkaldic War had broken out between Charles and the German Protestant princes. The Schmalkaldic League was seeking aid from both England and France, but Francis was reluctant to risk open support. For the moment, he wanted to concentrate his effort on recovering Boulogne.

Henry VIII's death in January 1547 could have given Francis an opportunity to realise this ambition, but he himself had only two more months to live. On his death-bed he is reputed to have told his son that he regretted damaging the kingdom by going to war on trivial pretexts and harming the cause of Christendom.

A final assessment of his foreign policy shows very little of lasting value. Francis's ambition to win back Milan was unrealistic, and led to a huge cost of both lives and money. His view of Charles as a threat was greatly exaggerated; Charles had far too many problems controlling his large dominions, nor was he the land-hungry aggressor that Francis imagined. Francis's dying comment is near the truth.

Francis I's foreign policy

7.1 A contemporary account

From Francesco Guicciardini's History of Italy, *Book 15, 1536*

For in our age methods of warfare have undergone the greatest changes: in that before King Charles of France marched into Italy, the brunt of battle was borne much more by horsemen heavily armed at all points, than by foot-soldiers; and since the weapons that were used against the towns were very difficult to move and manage, therefore, although armies frequently engaged in battles, there was very little killing, and most rare was the blood that was shed, and the cities under attack defended themselves so easily (not because of skilful defence but because of the lack of skill of the attack) that there was no town so weak or so small that it could not hold out for many days against the greatest armies of their enemies; with the result that only with the greatest difficulties could one make armed seizure of states belonging to others.

But after King Charles had come to Italy, the terror of unknown nations, the ferocity of infantry organised in waging war in another way, but above all, the fury of the artillery, filled all of Italy with so much dread that no hope of defending oneself remained for those not powerful enough to resist in the countryside . . .

Then terrified by the ferocity of the attacks, men began to whet theirs wits and contrive more subtle means of defence, fortifying their towns with banks, ditches, moats, flanks, ramparts, bastions; whence (the greater number of infantry pieces also helping to this purpose very much, more effective in defence than in attack) the towns now being defended have been made very safe and cannot be taken by storm.

Source: Francesco Guicciardini, *History of Italy*, translated by S. Alexander, London, 1969

7.2 Guicciardini comments on the events of 1519

From Francesco Guicciardini's History of Italy, *Book 13, 1536*

. . . and although he (the Emperor) was not as well provided with money as the king of France, nevertheless his power of furnishing armies with German and Spanish infantry was considered of greatest importance, since these were foot soldiers of the highest valour and reputation. But the contrary was true with regard to the king of France, because not having in his realm infantrymen to oppose the others, he could not involve himself in powerful wars except by gathering up foot soldiers from foreign countries at the greatest expense and sometimes with greatest difficulty. Therefore he was obliged to deal cautiously with the Swiss at great cost, and tolerate much of their insolence, and yet he was never entirely sure either of their constancy or of their fidelity . . . Nor did any doubt that between two princes, both young and with many reasons for rivalry and contention, a most serious war must inevitably result.

Source: Francesco Guicciardini, *History of Italy*, translated by S. Alexander, London, 1969

7.3 The French artillery

From Francesco Guicciardini's History of Italy, *Book 13, 1536*

They [the French guns] were planted against the walls of a town with such speed, the space between the shots was so little, and the balls flew so quickly and were impelled with such force, that as much execution was done in a few hours as formerly, in Italy, in the like number of days.

Source: Francesco Guicciardini, *History of Italy*, translated by S. Alexander, London, 1969

Document case-study questions

1 What is the meaning of 'flanks', 'ramparts' and 'bastions' in 7.1?

2 Why was Guicciardini deeply concerned with new methods of attacking and defending towns?

3 Is the author's assessment of the comparative strengths and weaknesses of Charles's and Francis's armies in 7.2 accurate?

4 What are the main changes in methods of warfare described in these three extracts and their implications?

5 How far do they help to explain the successes and failures of Francis's successive Italian campaigns?

Francis I and the pope

7.4 The Concordat of Bologna, 1516

An agreement made between Francis I and Pope Leo X

We order and decree henceforth, for all future times, in place of the said Pragmatic Sanction and all and singular chapters contained in it, as follows. In future, when any cathedrals or metropolitan sees in the said kingdom . . . shall fall vacant . . . their chapters and canons shall not be entitled to proceed to the election or postulation of the new prelate. In the event of such a vacancy, the King of France for the time being shall within six months . . . present and nominate to us and our successors as Bishops of Rome, or to the Holy See, a sober and knowledgeable master or graduate in theology . . . taught and rigorously examined at a reputable university, who must be at least twenty seven years old and otherwise suitable. And the person so nominated by the king shall be provided by us and our successors, or by the Holy See. And should the king fail to nominate a person so qualified, neither we nor our successors, nor the Holy See, shall be obliged to invest such a person. Within three months of our rejection of an unqualified person . . . the king shall be bound to nominate another candidate qualified as set out above. Failing which, considering the need to proceed swiftly in such burdensome vacancies, we and our successors, or the Holy See shall be at liberty to provide a person qualified as stated.

Source: R. J. Knecht, *French Renaissance monarchy: Francis I and Henry II*, London, 1984

Document case-study questions

6 Explain the two different meanings of the word 'chapters' in lines 2 and 4 in 7.4.

7 Explain the term 'Holy See' in 7.4, and indicate its role in the choice of candidates for ecclesiastical posts in France.

8 How does the Concordat try to ensure that only suitable candidates are selected?

9 Why was Francis willing to make a new agreement in place of the Pragmatic Constitution (or Sanction) at this time?

10 What is the significance of the Concordat of Bologna in relation to

a) Francis's extension of the power of the monarchy

b) Francis's attitude to Protestant reformers?

8 Francis I: religion

Francis's attitude to the church

Kings of France promised at their coronations to maintain the Roman Catholic church. The ceremony of their consecration set them aside from other laymen, and they took the title of 'Most Christian King'. Francis, like his predecessors, took this obligation very seriously. Although he was not a particularly devout or morally upright man, he felt committed to defend the church. He believed that the unity of the kingdom needed to be underpinned by religious unity, and used his royal patronage to make sure that men who supported him were appointed to all the top church posts within France. This control was officially recognised and reinforced by the Concordat of Bologna between Francis and the pope.

Religious change in France

The humanist movement

While people grumbled at the current state of the church, no one yet contemplated abandoning religion, or setting up a rival to Roman Catholicism. A few scholars (who became known as 'humanists') began to see a way to revitalise the church through a return to the Bible and to fresh study of the ancient Greek philosophers. Their work made them realise how later teachings had often distorted the church's message and this led them into conflict with men who had benefited from such changes. Meanwhile, the invention of printing meant that new ideas could reach a wide audience far more speedily.

The humanists had started to make an impact well before Francis came to the throne. Two of them stand out in particular. Jacques Lefèvre d'Etaples was a shy scholar who hoped that a reform of the way theology was taught would lead to reform of the church as a whole. Guillaume Briçonnet was a bishop who wanted to bring religion more effectively into people's lives. Both these men worked in the diocese of Meaux, and invited like-minded churchmen to join them. This group became known as the Meaux Circle, and was keenly supported by the king's sister, Marguerite. It soon ran into trouble with well-established clergy who saw these reformers as a threat, and tried to have them branded as heretics.

The reaction to Lutheranism

The Sorbonne, the theological faculty of the University of Paris, was expected to act as arbitrator in religious disputes. Like many long-established bodies, the Sorbonne tended to support existing practices and to oppose change. Not long afterwards, the Sorbonne was asked its opinion on a far more serious case of possible heresy; in 1517, Luther had published his attack on the papacy, followed by a spate of other pamphlets. Within two years, these were selling fast in Paris and the Sorbonne was invited to judge whether they were heretical. It took a long time over its deliberations and, in the meantime, Luther further defined his beliefs. By 1521, the Sorbonne was ready to condemn his works. The Paris *Parlement* had the task of enforcing the decree, but people took little notice of its demand that all Luther's works were to be handed in. Yet, from that time onwards, any Frenchman who criticised the church could be accused of sympathy with Luther, and thus of heresy.

Francis's attitude to the reformers

Francis faced a dilemma. He had no doubts about his opposition to Luther, but he wanted to protect the humanist scholars who had given him a reputation as a discerning patron of letters. When a promising young scholar, Louis de Berquin, came under the Sorbonne's scrutiny, Francis intervened to have him released from a heresy charge. Other members of the Meaux Circle also benefited from the king's protection, and Lefèvre d'Etaples' recent French translation of the New Testament was reprieved from the official ban of the church authorities.

They were soon in danger again, because of Francis's captivity after the Battle of Pavia. On his return to France, however, they too were released or came home from exile. Nonetheless, the Sorbonne was determined to go on harrying Berquin and a fresh commission was appointed to examine him. While the king was away in 1528, Berquin was found guilty of heresy and condemned to be burnt.

Francis's protection of humanist scholars did not mean he had any sympathy for what he considered to be real heresy. When religious dissidents hacked down a statue of the Virgin and Child, the king made public his outrage and his determination to have the culprits punished.

The growth of hard-line Protestantism

Radical ideas

Francis's change of attitude from 1533 to 1544 reflected the growth of radical ideas within the reform movement. In the early years of his reign, it was Luther's teaching that influenced many of those who were keen to see the church reform itself. By the end of the 1520s, the more radical ideas of Swiss reformers, such as Zwingli, were gaining support. Seeing no hope of renewal within the Roman Catholic church itself, the German and Swiss reformers were, by now, establishing completely new churches. Christianity in the West had started to break up, and these new churches threatened the religious uniformity that was regarded by many as the essential basis of national unity.

Guillaume Farel (originally a member of the Meaux Circle) had begun to set up a base in Switzerland from which to campaign for the conversion of France to his beliefs. Anyone who valued the unity of Western Christendom was bound to be alarmed. In 1533, the Sorbonne lodged a complaint against a sermon preached by the new rector of the university, Nicholas Cop. He was accused of sharing Lefèvre d'Etaples' ideas and of being influenced by Luther. Since this might lead to a heresy charge, he prudently fled. His friend, John Calvin, left Paris soon after, and the two men eventually chose Switzerland as their refuge. Francis agreed to sanction a short period of persecution, to limit any damage. At that point, he was negotiating the marriage of his son to the pope's niece, Catherine de' Medici, and was keen to enhance his reputation as a zealous Catholic.

The Affair of the Placards

In 1533, those suspected of heresy were merely arrested; a year later, far worse awaited them. This was the year of the much-misinterpreted Affair of the Placards. Today it would be called a poster campaign; one night a group of radical reformers stuck up posters in the streets of Paris and five other towns, and also on the royal palace at Amboise.

It was later discovered that these had been composed and printed at Farel's headquarters in Switzerland. The posters' message was a violent attack on the Mass, the central service of the Roman Catholic church. It went far beyond anything Luther's followers would have countenanced, attacking in abusive language the belief in Transubstantiation.* This was a crude reflection of Zwingli's teaching that the service re-creating Christ's Last Supper was purely an act of commemoration. Until then, anyone in France proposing church reform had been labelled a Lutheran; from now on, this was clearly a gross over-simplification.

Yet these posters could be used by the church to provide proof that every reformer was out to undermine the most basic beliefs of all Christians. They were a godsend to those who wished to crush all types of reform, from the mild criticisms of the humanist scholars to the more radical demands of the Lutherans and the even stronger attacks of Zwingli's followers. Up until now, Francis had made a distinction between the scholars (whose criticisms of the church deserved toleration), and those who attacked Catholic beliefs (who had to be silenced).

The immediate reaction to the posters was hysterical. Rumours flew round Paris that the reformers were plotting to burn down churches and massacre congregations at Mass. Francis shared the general outrage, and supported *Parlement* in its response. This time, suspected heretics were imprisoned and

---

*Roman Catholic doctrine that, in the Mass, the priest's blessing changed the substance of the bread and wine into the body and blood of Christ; the outward appearance or 'accidents' remained unaltered.

many were burnt. All book printing was banned and huge public demonstrations were organised through the streets of Paris, with the king taking part.

Persecution as a permanent policy

Now that a few reformers had shown how far they would go in attacking Catholic beliefs, the king felt he could no longer support any degree of toleration and keep his claim to be 'The Most Christian King'. From now on, there would be an all-out campaign to crush every form of heresy in France. Unlike Henry VIII, Francis had no political motive to break with Rome: the church in France was already under firm royal control.

The new wave of persecution came at an awkward time for Francis's foreign policy. He had started to cultivate the friendship of the German Protestants as possible allies against Charles V. Not surprisingly, they were put off by news of the burnings in France. To soothe them, Francis issued, in 1535, a statement claiming that the persecution had political, not religious motives. They were unconvinced, even when he produced an edict ending persecution on the grounds that heresy had been stamped out. But the supporters of Zwingli (known as Sacramentarians in France) were excepted, and others were only offered a pardon if they renounced their Protestant beliefs within six months. If not, they faced hanging.

In 1538, Francis made peace with Charles V, and no longer needed to win the friendship of the German Protestant princes. Persecution had not destroyed the French Protestants, and the courts asked for increased powers to find and punish them. The Edict of Fontainebleau, issued in 1540, gave the *Parlements* the right to seek out heretics and all citizens were instructed to assist in this task. In 1543 the Sorbonne made it easier to identify heresy by publishing a list of 25 basic points of Catholic belief and practice. This was issued as a law with the force of royal power behind it. Closer control of books was another weapon against heresy, and many titles were banned.

Calvinism after 1541

The spread of Calvinism

Despite all these efforts, the reform movement never stopped growing in France. From 1541, the ideas of John Calvin began to make an impact. Calvin had fled to Switzerland in 1534. There he completed his great book *The institutes of the Christian religion*, with which he hoped to convert all Frenchmen and, indeed, all the world to his views. He even dedicated the book to Francis.

The impact of Luther's ideas had resulted in the creation of a new church in Germany, but it needed the conversion of the ruler in order to establish itself in any new location. Calvinism was different; it could spread as an underground movement in countries where the government opposed it, setting up small secret groups of dedicated members who were ready to risk death for their beliefs. It was suited in every way to lead the spread of Protestantism in the second stage of the Reformation, when Lutheranism had lost its original energy.

Unlike the Lutherans, Calvin's followers had everything needed for a new church set out with great clarity in one book. Once *The institutes* was published in Basle in 1536, Calvinism was unstoppable. Calvin continually revised and expanded it, translating the original Latin version into French in 1541. Copies poured into France; the Sorbonne outlawed it and publicly burned piles of copies, but more kept on arriving.

Calvin had learnt the mechanism of establishing a new church while he was in temporary exile in Strassburg (at that time part of the Holy Roman Empire). During his far longer residence in Geneva, he was able to refine his methods. Here he set up a missionary base for the new church, and a place where refugees from persecution in France could live in safety.

Many of these fugitives had received a summons to appear before a royal court on a heresy charge (suspects were given three days' notice). By the 1540s, almost all heresy cases came up before royal, not church courts, on the grounds that the accused were a threat to public order as well as religious orthodoxy. Torture was frequently used to extract confessions, and the punishments ranged from confiscation of property to death by burning.

It is hardly surprising that, by 1560, somewhere between 5,000 to 10,000 French citizens had gone to Geneva. (The exact number is impossible to calculate.) A similar number had stayed in France and undergone trial for heresy. Around 7 per cent of these had been sentenced to burning; the majority were fined or imprisoned.

These totals take us well beyond the end of Francis's reign, for which separate national figures do not exist. But, by the time he died in 1547, Calvinism was making rapid advances in France, in spite of all the efforts at suppression. It was poised to take the next step, the establishment of fixed congregations with their own ministers and their own form of service.

Calvin's appeal to the French

Who were these French men and women who were willing to risk persecution for the sake of their new faith? Since the Bible was the basis of the new church's authority, it only appealed to literate people. This excluded the really poor, and the bulk of country dwellers. Calvinism also attracted those who had very little say in the affairs of church or state, but who wanted to have a greater share. But it was not only the French middle class that was attracted to Calvinism; it also had many converts among the aristocracy. Here, there was deep resentment at the growth of royal power, and embracing an illegal religion was one way of expressing this. The separate, self-governing Calvinist congregations often found safety in a nobleman's house; but, in Francis's time, they were still meeting informally.

The failure of suppression

The state of religion in France was very different in 1547 from what it had been in 1515, and was on the threshold of even greater changes. Under Francis's son and grandson, Calvinism would emerge as a powerful new force, and the attempts to suppress it would lead to prolonged civil war. Francis had tried to distinguish between those who wished to reform the existing church and those who wanted to break away from it. Eventually, radical Protestantism forced him towards an attempt at total suppression. But, by then, the tide of change was running too strongly, and no amount of effort by state and church could prevent the break-up of the religious unity the king prized.

Document case study
Francis I and religion

8.1 The need for reform

Jacques Lefèvre d'Etaples, writing in his Commentarii initiatorii in IV Evangilis praefatio, *1522*

Why may we not aspire to see our age restored to the likeness of the primitive Church, when Christ received a purer veneration, and the splendour of his name shone forth more widely?. . . As the light of the Gospel returns, may He Who is blessed above all grant also to us this increase of faith, this purity of worship . . . The knowledge of languages, and especially of Latin and Greek . . . began to return about the time when Constantinople was captured by the enemies of Christ, when a few Greeks . . . took refuge in Italy . . . Would that the name of Christ might have been, and may henceforth be, proclaimed purely and sincerely so that soon the word may be fulfilled: 'O, Lord, may the whole earth adore Thee'. Yes, may it offer Thee a religion evangelical and pure, a religion of the spirit and of truth!

Source: Jacques Lefèvre d'Etaples, *Commentarii initiatorii in IV Evangilis praefatio*, 1522, M. McLauglin and J. B. Ross (eds.), London, 1953

8.2 Cop calls for men to speak the truth at any cost

Part of a sermon preached by Nicholas Cop, Rector of the University of Paris and close friend of Calvin, in November 1533. Cop and Calvin fled into exile immediately afterwards.

Why then do we conceal the truth rather than speak it boldly? Is it right to please men rather than God, to fear those who can destroy the body but not the soul? . . . The world and the wicked are wont to label as heretics, impostors, seducers and evil-speakers those who strive purely and sincerely to penetrate the minds of believers with the Gospel . . . But happy and blessed are they who endure all this with composure, giving thanks to God in the midst of affliction and bravely bearing calamities.

Source: 'Joannis Calvin Opera IX' translated by D. Cooper and F. L. Battles in *The Hartford Quarterly*, vol. VI, 1965

8.3 The Affair of the Placards

Criticism of the doctrine of the Mass from the Placard of October 1534

True articles on the horrible, great and insufferable papal Mass devised in direct opposition to the Last Supper.

I call on heaven and earth to bear witness to the truth against this pompous and proud papal Mass by which the world (unless God soon provides a remedy) is being and will be completely destroyed, and in which our Lord is so outrageously blasphemed and the people seduced and blinded.

First, every faithful Christian must know that our Lord and Saviour, Jesus Christ, has given his body, life and blood for our sanctification in a perfect sacrifice. This cannot be repeated . . . yet the world is still crowded in many places with wretched sacrificers, who, setting themselves up as our redeemers, take the place of Jesus Christ or profess to be his companions.

Secondly, through this wretched Mass almost every one is being led into public idolatry, for it is falsely claimed that Jesus Christ is bodily present in the bread and wine. Not only is this not taught by Holy Scripture and our faith, for Jesus Christ after his resurrection went to heaven . . . it follows that if his body is in heaven, He is not on earth.

Thirdly, these wretched sacrificers, compounding their error, claim that once they have whispered or spoken over the bread and wine these disappear, and that through Transubstantiation (such is their fondness for long and inflated words!) Jesus Christ is concealed within the accidents of the bread and the wine. This is the doctrine of devils and contrary to Scripture.

Fourthly, the product of the Mass is quite unlike that of the Last Supper, which is not miraculous . . . The product of the Last Supper is to proclaim one's faith and certainty in salvation and to remember the death and passion of Jesus Christ . . . But the product of the Mass is quite otherwise: for all knowledge of Jesus Christ is wiped out, the Gospel is not preached and time is taken up with bell-ringing, howling, chanting, ceremonies, censings, disguises and all manner of monkey-tricks whereby the people, like lambs and sheep, are led astray and devoured by these ravenous wolves.

Source: R. J. Knecht, *Renaissance warrior and patron*, Cambridge, 1994

8.4 Francis's reaction to the Placards

A speech by Francis I in January 1535, after he had taken part in a religious procession through Paris. Six heretics were burnt on that day.

The king began by claiming that France was the only country which had not nourished religious monsters, but there were now 'wicked and unfortunate persons who wished to spoil her good name, sowing damnable and execrable opinions . . . I rejoice in the piety, good zeal and affection which I read in your faces . . . Our fathers have shown us how to live according to the doctrine of God and Holy Mother Church, in which I hope to live and die . . . I would see the errors chased out of my kingdom and no one excused, in such sort that if one of my arms were infected by this corruption I would cut it off. And were my children stained by it, I would myself burn them.'

Source: R. J. Knecht, *Renaissance warrior and patron*, Cambridge, 1994

Document case-study questions

1 What is the meaning of 'blasphemed', 'idolatry' and 'accidents' in 8.3?

2 Explain the significance of the 'knowledge of languages, and especially Latin and Greek' in 8.1 in restoring the importance of the Bible at this time.

3 What emphasis is placed on knowledge of the Gospel in the first three documents? What other authority is given in 8.4?

4 In the light of views expressed in 8.2, were the king's threats in 8.4 likely to be effective in stamping out heresy?

5 Compare the tone of 8.1 and 8.2 with that of 8.3, and suggest why the latter caused such outrage.

6 Using all four documents, explain why the king's attitude to religious reform changed between 8.1 (1522) and 8.2 (1533).

9 Francis I as patron of arts and letters

Francis's motives as patron

The motives of any patron are likely to be complex, and will include a genuine love of art, and a desire for self-publicity, in varying proportions. In the case of the Renaissance monarchs, there was a further political dimension; patronage of the arts and of letters was used as a means of enhancing the image of power of both the individual ruler and the state.

Francis I was a cultivated man who enjoyed having beautiful paintings on the walls of his palaces and learned scholars collecting books for his library. He was also acutely aware how a skilful artist could project him as a strong king, a handsome warrior and a man of taste. Henry VIII and Charles V were equally adept at using art as propaganda to enhance their prestige, and the three men, all much of an age, competed in self-projection through patronage of arts and letters.

The influence of the Italian Renaissance had been felt in France well before Francis's accession. Humanist scholars had begun to have influence; Italian painters and architects were acknowledged as the best in Europe. The Frenchmen who accompanied Charles VIII and Louis XII on their Italian campaigns had seen the beauty, as well as the riches of Italy, and begun to covet the paintings and statues, the clothes and palaces that created the luxury of an Italian Renaissance court.

Francis intended to create a court as cultured and magnificent as those of the popes and the rulers of Milan, Ferrara or Florence. Centralisation of administration within the kingdom was echoed by the court's ambition to lead the country's culture as well. Nobles sought to keep up with the royal example by building châteaux in the Italian style, and collecting works of art. The wealthiest merchants and financiers were quick to follow.

Italian architectural influence

The Château of Blois

Before Francis came to the throne, the occasional Italian craftsmen had been invited to France to add Renaissance features to a tomb, a church or a château. It was the king, however, who brought Italian Renaissance architecture to France in a big way. The Château of Blois was his first project; just after his accession he ordered a new wing for the great royal castle overlooking the River Loire. He wanted this to fit into the existing medieval castle, and even rest on foundations already in place, so it could not be a purely Italianate creation.

The most striking feature of Francis's new wing is its staircase. Here, a traditional design for a spiral staircase was transformed into an elaborate Renaissance porch. The face of the new wing overlooking the town of Blois is equally original, with a two-storey arcaded loggia running all along it, based on a design used to extend the Vatican a few years earlier.

The writer, La Fontaine, wrote later how 'the part built by Francis I, seen from the outside, pleased me more than anything else. There are many little galleries, little windows, little balconies, little ornaments without regularity or order; these make up a whole which is big and rather pleasing.' He had spotted the essence of French adaptation of Italian design: it borrowed all sorts of individual features, but combined them together in haphazard fashion. This was in contrast to the process of selecting and balancing them to create an ordered whole, as in a perfect example of a Renaissance building in Italy.

The Château of Chambord

Chambord, which is further up the Loire from Blois, is the most famous of Francis's completely new buildings. It is set back some way from the river in the forest where the king loved to hunt. Although it is vast, it was intended as a hunting lodge where the king could come for a while with a handful of companions, rather than as a longer-term residence for the whole court.

Francis first ordered work to start at Chambord in 1519, but there were long delays while he was away from France. It was only ready for use in the last years of his reign (and not completed till after his death). The original architect was almost certainly an Italian, Domenico da Cortona, but he had followed the

The Château of Chambord, sixteenth century.

ground plan of a typical medieval castle, with a square central courtyard and towers at each corner. Within this, lies a keep in the unusual shape of a Greek cross, an idea that was probably borrowed from Lorenzo de' Medici's villa at Poggio a Caiano. This had been designed by Giuliano da Sangallo, of whom da Cortona was a pupil.

There is an extraordinary double spiral staircase in the centre of Chambord's cross-shaped keep, providing separate sets of stairs for going up and coming down. This was not in Domenico's original design. Here, and in many other parts, the French builders adapted the plans to bring them into the tradition with which these craftsmen were more familiar. It could also work the other way round. The original French idea, for example, was for a series of turrets up on the roof, but the individual miniature towers are decorated with all sorts of pure Italian features. Chambord is a French–Italian hybrid, but the overall impact is more French than Italian.

The spread of the Renaissance style in France

But it was the Italian features that Francis's courtiers wanted to copy in their own homes. Chenonceaux, Azay-le-Rideaux and other châteaux sprang up along the Loire, as aristocrats and rich bourgeois vied with each other to display their wealth and their taste. In Francis's last years, further afield, in Paris and in northern France, the architects Pierre Lescot and Philibert de l'Orme were designing in the Renaissance style.

Fontainebleau

After Francis's imprisonment in Spain he spent more time in the Paris area than in the Loire valley. Since there was no suitable royal palace for the lavish life-style the king wished to lead, he first commissioned the Château de Madrid on the outskirts of Paris (now destroyed), and then started to enlarge his property at Fontainebleau. As at Blois, the new building had to fit in with an existing medieval base. In 1528, the king commissioned a French master mason, Gilles Le Breton, to build a new gatehouse, a long gallery, and probably also the large courtyard now called the Cour des Adieux. Le Breton used Italian decorative features with a considerable feeling for the style of classical buildings, but Francis was soon using a native Italian to supervise further additions at Fontainebleau. This was Serlio, author of a famous treatise on architecture, which became the inspiration for countless great houses all over France and England as well as Italy. Serlio's books contained hundreds of drawings that could be adapted for inclusion in any building. It became the height of sophistication for architects to include Serlian doorways, fireplaces, and windows in their designs.

Serlio dedicated a volume to Francis, and then another, and was rewarded in 1541 with an invitation to take over supervision of the building works at Fontainebleau. But he never used this position to make a big impact on the design of the palace; his real influence consisted in making Frenchmen aware of the achievements of Italian architects.

Painting: the school of Fontainebleau

Two other Italians invited by Francis made a more definite contribution to the king's plans. Giovanni Battista Rosso and Francesco Primaticcio were responsible for the interior decoration of many important rooms with paintings and stucco; unfortunately many have been destroyed in later re-modellings of the palace. Primaticcio's nymphs still stretch their graceful limbs around the central panel of the mantelpiece in the *Chambre de la reine* and the *Chambre de la duchesse d'Etampes*. (Other works of his at Fontainebleau date from the next reign.) But the main survival is Rosso's magnificent *Galerie François Premier*, lined with painted panels surrounded by stucco figures, each portraying a mythical scene. Between them, Primaticcio and Rosso had transformed French art, creating what came to be known as the School of Fontainebleau, with its Mannerist style of elongated figures and heads with exaggeratedly classical profiles.

In Francis's time, the king's bath house lay underneath this gallery and was equally prized. Again, the walls were decorated with paint and stucco. It was here, also, that the king chose to display the best pictures in his collection as he wanted his pictures in the room where he spent some of his most pleasurable hours. For French aristocrats, whose homes were draughty stone castles, Fontainebleau, with its rich tapestries, pictures and panelling, must have seemed exotic beyond belief.

Italian artists invited to France

Primaticcio had been sent to Rome in 1540 to collect works of art for Francis, including moulds for many famous Renaissance bronze statues. The king already had the pictures that had come to France with Leonardo da Vinci after the capture of Milan in 1515, such as the *Mona Lisa* and the *Virgin of the rocks*. He had hoped that the great artist would continue to work for him after he was settled in the modest Château of Cloux near the royal palace at Amboise. But Leonardo was old and sick, and there is no proof that he did any work for Francis in the three years he spent at Cloux before he died.

Soon after this, the Florentine painter, Andrea del Sarto, visited France and painted Francis's baby son, returning to Italy with cash to buy pictures for the king. Throughout his reign, Francis commissioned agents to search Italy for paintings and statues to enhance the royal collection. In 1538, the king invited Titian to visit him, stimulated by the arrival of a portrait of Francis portraying the king as a broad-shouldered, masterful figure (which had been painted from a medal, not from life). However, the artist could not be tempted to leave Venice. Michelangelo also declined an invitation to France, but his statue of Hercules was set up in the grounds at Fontainebleau.

News of Francis's bounty as a patron also attracted to France the sculptor and goldsmith Benvenuto Cellini. His pursuit of the king was finally rewarded by several commissions and the provision of a fine studio in Paris. Benvenuto stayed in France for five years, creating enormous and costly works in precious metals, which Francis would come to see while they were being made. The most famous to survive is a vast and ornate golden salt-cellar, now in Vienna.

Jean Clouet's portraits

The work of Italian painters, sculptors and architects became the height of fashion in Francis's time, but the first choice for portraits was an artist nearer home. This was Jean Clouet, who was probably born in Flanders, but spent most of his life in France. As court painter, he made many drawings of the king and leading figures at court, some of which were used as the basis for paintings. His work resembles that of Holbein, who was in England at the same time. Both men produced likenesses of astonishing realism, although their drawing techniques were different.

The establishment of a humanist college

Francis's patronage extended to learning as well as the arts. He was well aware that, in this way, he could enhance the prestige of France as well as of himself. We have already seen his protection of humanist scholars against accusations of heresy. Guillaume Budé, Francis's secretary, who had taught himself Greek and written two books on classical subjects, encouraged his master to be generous to scholars. Two years after Marignano, the king wanted to show the world that he was not only a great soldier, but also a man of learning and taste, so in 1517 he announced that he wished to establish a college for the study of classical languages. Erasmus, by now the most famous humanist scholar in Europe, was invited to become its first principal. He would have brought great prestige to the new foundation, but he turned down the offer as he did not wish to be tied to one place or one patron. Instead, Francis invited John Lascaris, a native Greek, who was head of a similar college in Rome. Another delay was caused by disagreement over what combination of the Greek, Latin or Hebrew languages the college should teach. By now, the prolonged negotiations had sapped Francis's enthusiasm. He decided to set up the college in Milan instead of Paris, and dispatched Lascaris to find premises and recruit students. Lascaris also went to Venice and found time to acquire Greek manuscripts for Francis's library at Blois.

Meanwhile, Budé tried to keep the king's interest alive. When Francis found he could not understand a letter from Lascaris because it was written in Greek, Budé took the chance to point out how urgently more knowledge of Greek was needed in France. Francis responded by proclaiming that eight scholars would be appointed to teach Greek in Paris. The unfortunate Lascaris was abandoned; no more money reached him from France, and when his pleas for help went unanswered, he closed his college.

Libraries and printing

At the same time, Francis created a new post of Master of the King's Library, and gave it to Budé. A few years later, a *Lecteur du roi* was appointed to read aloud to the king. The king also encouraged printing by appointing a king's printer for Hebrew, Latin and Greek, and subsidising the creation of fonts of Greek type. An ordinance of 1537 ordered that one copy of every printed book should be given to the library at Blois. Francis ordered his agents to buy precious books and manuscripts from all over Europe. Consequently, he was able to build up a second library at Fontainebleau and also a small collection to accompany him on his travels. This included Roman history, as well as lighter reading, and the king took the trouble to make himself well acquainted with its contents.

Francis eventually moved his whole collection to Fontainebleau and, much later, it became the foundation of the *Bibliothèque nationale*, the French equivalent of the British Library. His patronage of learning and the arts was no window-dressing exercise, but the achievement of a man with a genuine interest in and appreciation of books and works of art. During his reign, the Italian Renaissance made a wide impact on France, and her prestige increased in the eyes of western Europe. Francis did not reach Henry VIII's level of musical expertise, but he took an interest in attracting singers and players of high quality to perform at court. In all other respects, he was able to outshine the ruler he regarded as a rival in this sphere as well as in war.

Document case study
Francis I as patron of the arts

9.1 Niccolò Alamanni is ordered to find Italian paintings

Letter from Niccolò Alamanni to Francesco Gonzaga, marquis of Mantua, June 1504:

As I am the servant and familiar of our little prince of Angoulême, he has expressed the wish that I should obtain for him some pictures of those excellent Italian masters, as they give him so much pleasure. Since I know that M. Andrea Mantegna is among the best, and also that he is liked by your Lordship, I take the liberty of writing to beg you to cause M. Mantegna . . . to make him something exceptional . . . I have sent orders to Florence and elsewhere for others to be made.

Source: D. Seward, *Prince of the Renaissance*, London, 1973

9.2 Francis's first meeting with Cellini

Cellini, writing in his autobiography

I crossed the river and waited upon his Majesty. He was quite gracious to me and asked if I had anything lovely to show him. I replied that as for loveliness I was not so sure, but I had done some work with great study and with all the devotion that so noble an art demanded, and that if it was good it was due to him who allowed me to want for nothing, such freehandedness being the only way of getting the best work done. [The King was then invited to visit Benvenuto's studio and shown his latest work; the artist placed Francis so that he would see the statue in the best light and ordered his apprentice to let down a curtain.] 'Instantly the King raised his hands and spoke in my praise the most complimentary words that human tongue ever uttered'.

Source: *The life of Benvenuto Cellini written by himself*, translated by J. A. Symonds, ed. J. Pope-Hennessy, London, 1949.

9.3 Another encounter between Francis and Cellini

The king's words as recorded in Cellini's autobiography

There is one important matter, Benvenuto, which men of your sort, though full of talent, ought always to bear in mind; it is that you cannot bring your great gifts to light by your own strength alone; you show your greatness only through the opportunities we give you. You have chosen to execute a salt-cellar, and vases and busts and doors . . . which quite confound me, when I consider how you have neglected my wishes and worked for the fulfilment of your own . . . I tell you, therefore, plainly: do your utmost to obey my commands; for if you stick to your own fancies you will run your head against a wall.

Source: *The life of Benvenuto Cellini written by himself*, translated by J. A. Symonds, ed. J. Pope-Hennessy, London, 1949.

Document case-study questions

1 Identify 'our little prince of Angoulême' and 'M. Andrea Mantegna'.

2 Why would Italian paintings be sought after by a French collector in 1504?

3 Contrast the tone of 9.2 and 9.3 and suggest a reason.

4 Explain the king's attitude to patronage expressed in 9.3; how and why is it echoed in Cellini's reply to the king in 9.2?

5 What do all three documents reveal about Francis's interest in the arts and its limitations?

Conclusion

When Niccolò Machiavelli sat down to write *The prince* in 1514, he was painfully aware of the weakness of the Italian states. He had seen his homeland become the battleground on which larger neighbours – Spain, France and the Holy Roman Empire – fought out their rivalries. So he decided to write a book to offer rulers advice on how to build up the strength of their dominions through clever state-craft. Since this involved giving second place to moral considerations, his book acquired great notoriety.

Only two years later Erasmus wrote *The institution of a Christian prince* for young Charles, the future Holy Roman Emperor. Where Machiavelli's book looks forward to the modern world of power politics, Erasmus looks back to medieval ideas of kingship as a form of Christian duty, hemmed in by rights and obligations and with moral considerations coming first.

The Renaissance monarchs who form the subject of this book lived at a time of transition between the two worlds represented here by Erasmus and Machiavelli. They faced pressures from contrary directions, pushing them towards both the medieval and the modern concepts of a monarch's role. Each of them tried to work out a balance between the two.

Ferdinand and Isabella worked most closely with the church. In Isabella's case, she was deeply influenced by Christian morality in her relations with her subjects. Francis I put the advancement of his personal prestige and his country's power at the top of his agenda. Charles V faced the worst problems of all, and part of his failure to deal with the Lutherans came from his unwillingness to sacrifice his moral code to political demands until it was too late.

All these rulers worked tirelessly to strengthen the authority of the crown in their countries. In every case this involved the creation of new organs of central government; in Spain these were the royal councils with their special areas of responsibility. Charles V expanded on his predecessors' work in Spain, but was not able to create new institutions in his other territories that made up the Holy Roman Empire. Francis I overhauled the financial machinery in France and created new officials and bodies to achieve greater efficiency.

These monarchs increased the crown income substantially, but at a time of inflation and escalating costs they could not keep up with expenditure and sank deeply into debt. Each did his or her best to nourish the country's economy; Spain acquired the seemingly limitless riches of the New World and worked out a system of state monopoly and levy to syphon a substantial share into the royal coffers.

Each of these rulers had a strong sense of the need to protect national unity through the preservation of religious unity. In Spain this involved the suppression of Muslim and Jewish belief, in France and Germany it led to civil war with the Protestants and the eventual recognition of their right to worship freely. These monarchs were all willing to sacrifice awkward and overmighty subjects to the greater good of public order, justice and security, and their own power. They were also keen to extend royal control into new areas, such as church appointments and the regulation of overseas trade.

Yet the great nobles who had wielded so much power in the past were still strong, though in each country the rulers had called on the well-educated middle class to provide the workforce for their governments and systems of justice. As the new institutions grew confident, the holders of the medieval titles found their importance declining.

Change was at its most rapid in this period in the field of war. The size of armies was escalating; so was the potency of weapons, which inevitably changed the methods by which victories were won.

The need to raise more money to pay for these wars was the main stimulus to the development of better central government control of finance. Yet so many of the campaigns described in this book failed because the troops fell ill for lack of basic necessities such as clean water; the Middle Ages are still not far away.

Prowess in war remained a major source of prestige in this period, though none of the other monarchs fully shared Francis's aggressive search for personal glory. Ferdinand preferred to gain his territories through a mixture of diplomacy and military victory. To achieve this, he set up a network of ambassadors that provided him with contacts. This method was quickly copied by other countries.

Yet the simplest way to expand one's territories and influence was still through the old route of dynastic marriages. All these rulers used this tool with varying success – Charles V was perhaps the keenest on the preservation and expansion of his family. Many peace settlements were cemented with weddings.

The plea for peace in Erasmus' book received scant attention, except in the case of Charles V. The period saw many wars, as the great powers spent more and more of their resources to win control of parts of Italy or to wrest territory from their neighbours. The pattern of alliances shifts constantly as the one-time victor comes to be seen as a threat by his former friends, who then seek to establish a crude balance of power by changing sides.

With the exception of Charles V as Holy Roman Emperor (but not as king of Spain), each one of these rulers left his or her country a better governed, more united and wealthier state, with the authority of the crown considerably strengthened and the forces that could threaten it held in check.

Select bibliography

Ferdinand and Isabella

J. H. Elliott, *Imperial Spain*, London, 1983, provides in its first four chapters an invaluable analysis and account of these reigns. H. Kamen, *Spain 1416–1714*, 2nd edn, London, 1991, is a stimulating study of the same period. P. K. Liss, *Isabel the queen*, New York, 1992, provides a detailed and sympathetic biography of Isabella, but there is no equivalent in English on Ferdinand's life. G. Mattingly, *Renaissance diplomacy*, London, 1955, examines Ferdinand's diplomatic methods in the context of those of other contemporary rulers. J. Edwards, *The monarchies of Ferdinand and Isabella*, Historical Association, 1996, is a brief summary which includes comments on the latest research on the subject. There are a great many books on Spain's overseas empire. J. H. Parry, *Europe and the wider world*, London, 1949, and *The age of Renaissance*, London, 1963, are general surveys that include admirable coverage of Spain.

Charles V

The books by J. H. Elliott and H. Kamen cited above are also extremely useful for their chapters on Charles as king of Spain. F. Fernandez Armesto, *Columbus*, Oxford, 1991, is a reliable and lively biography. J. Lynch, *Spain under the Hapsburgs*, vol. I, Oxford, 1965, covers the reign in greater detail and includes useful material on the geographical, social and economic background. K. Brandi, *Charles V*, London, 1939, remains the fullest biography available in English. M. Fernandez Alvarez, *Charles V: elected emperor and hereditary ruler*, London, 1975, is much shorter but gives a vivid personal portrait of the man. M. Rady, *Charles V*, London, 1988, is a very useful short account with special emphasis on Charles and Germany. H. G. Koenigsberger, 'The Emperor Charles V', *History Sixth* , vol. 4, May 1989, gives a concise survey based on the author's chapter in *The new Cambridge modern history*, vol. II, Cambridge, 1990. M. Hughes, *Early modern Germany*, London, 1992, gives a useful and clear introduction to the problems facing Charles. Charles's contest with Luther and his followers is covered in all the books on the Reformation, and any biographies of Martin Luther. G. R. Elton, *Reformation Europe*, London, 1963, is an excellent survey. Useful collections of documents can be found in 'Martin Luther', *Documents of modern history*, E. G. Rupp and B. Drewery (eds.), London, 1970; K. Leach, *Documents and debates series: sixteenth-century Europe*, London, 1980; and *Documents and debates series: the German Reformation*, London, 1991.

Francis I

R. Knecht, *Renaissance warrior and patron: the reign of Francis I*, Cambridge, 1994, provides by far the best biography in English. The author wrote the original book in 1982. He summarised it for students' use in *French Renaissance monarchy: Francis I and Henry II*, London, 1984, and expanded and revised it in 1994.

D. Seward, *Prince of the Renaissance, the life of Francis I*, London, 1973, is a lighter biography with plentiful illustrations. J. H. Shennan, *Government and society in France, 1461–1661*, London, 1969, considers the different views on the role of the monarch at that time. D. Potter, *A history of*

France, 1460–1560, London, 1995, includes useful analyses of French society and foreign policy. G. Parker, *The military revolution*, Cambridge, new edition 1996, provides fascinating detail on the changes in warfare that took place during this time. M. Greengrass, *The French Reformation*, Oxford, 1987, gives valuable information on the early stages of Calvinism. A. Blunt, *Art and architecture in France, 1500–1700*, Harmondsworth, 1957, is a scholarly art historian's account of the buildings and paintings of the period. A useful collection of documents is found in J. H. Shennan, *Government and society in France*, London, 1969.

Chronology

1469 The marriage takes place between Ferdinand of Aragon and Isabella of Castile.

1474 Isabella becomes queen of Castile.

1476 The *Cortes* of Madrigal begins to restore royal authority in Castile and the brotherhood of Santa Hermandad is revived to deal with bandits.

1478 Ferdinand and Isabella apply to Rome for permission to establish the Inquisition in Castile.

1479 Ferdinand becomes king of Aragon.

1480 The *Cortes* of Toledo passes the Act of Resumption, taking back revenues into crown hands. It establishes the restructured Royal Council of Castile as the central governing body of the country.

1482 Ferdinand and Isabella begin their campaign against the kingdom of Granada.

1489 Ferdinand of Aragon and Henry VII negotiate the Treaty of Medina del Campo. Ferdinand's daughter, Catherine, and Prince Arthur of England are betrothed.

1492 The city of Granada is captured and the *Reconquista* of Spain is completed.

1492 Columbus sets out on his first voyage to the West Indies.

1492 Ferdinand and Isabella order the expulsion of the Jews from Spain.

1494 Louise of Savoy gives birth to the future Francis I of France.

1494 The Treaty of Tordesillas between Spain and Portugal is signed. This divides the New World between Spain and Portugal along an imaginary line, 370 leagues west of the Cape Verde Islands.

1495 The French king, Charles VIII, enters Naples.

1495 Ferdinand of Aragon constructs a new Holy League, together with the papacy, the Holy Roman Empire and England. The Treaty of Venice, aimed at restoring Naples' independence, and excluding France permanently from Italy, is signed.

1500 Juana of Castile gives birth to the future Charles V.

1503 Spain defeats France at the Battle of Cerignola in Italy. The French are forced to recognise Spanish sovereignty over Sicily, Sardinia and Naples.

1503 The House of Trade is established in Seville.

1504 Queen Isabella of Castile dies.

1505 Ferdinand of Aragon signs the Treaty of Blois with Louis XII of France.

1506 Charles becomes ruler of the Netherlands after the death of his father, Philip of Burgundy.

1508 Ferdinand of Aragon joins the League of Cambrai against Venice.

1512 Ferdinand of Aragon occupies Navarre, which he eventually makes part of Castile.

1515 Francis I becomes king of France.

1515 Francis I invades Italy and captures Milan from the Sforzas after the Battle of Marignano.

1516 Francis I and Pope Leo X sign the Concordat of Bologna, ending a period of hostility between the papacy and the French kings.

1516 Charles of Burgundy becomes king of Spain on the death of his grandfather, Ferdinand of Aragon.

1516 Francis I and Charles V sign the Treaty of Noyon.

1517 Luther displays his 95 theses on the door of the Castle Church in Wittenberg.

1519 Charles V is elected Holy Roman Emperor.

1519 Charles V appoints Mercurino Gattinara as Grand Imperial Chancellor.

1520 Luther is excommunicated by Pope Leo X.

1520 Henry VIII and Francis I meet at the Field of the Cloth of Gold outside Ardres.

1520–22 The *Comunero* revolt breaks out. The inhabitants of the cities in northern Castile send a list of demands to Charles V. The rebels are defeated at the Battle of Villalar.

1521 The *Germanias*, a rising in Valencia and Mallorca, is crushed.

1521 Charles V calls the Diet of Worms. An Imperial edict places Luther under the Ban of the Empire. He retires to Elector Frederick of Saxony's castle, the Wartburg.

1521 Fighting breaks out between Francis I and Charles V for the first time.

1521 The Sorbonne in Paris condemns Luther's works.

1522 The Compact of Brussels makes Charles V's brother, Ferdinand, regent in Germany and gives him rule over all the Habsburg family lands in Germany and Austria.

1522 Charles V gains victory over the French at La Bicocca.

1523 The duke of Bourbon joins forces with Charles V. In his absence, he is found guilty of treason and his estates are confiscated by Francis I.

1523 Francis I begins the first wave of financial reforms in France.

1523 Charles V and his allies invade France.

1523 The humanist scholar, Lefèvre d'Etaples, publishes his translation of the New Testament in French.

1523 Francis I launches a new attack on Italy and appoints his mother, Louise of Savoy, regent in his absence.

1524 The Council of the Indies is set up to control Spain's transatlantic territories.

1525 Charles V defeats Francis at the Battle of Pavia. Francis I is captured and imprisoned.

1525 The Peasants' War breaks out. The movement has no real leaders, and the revolt collapses in the face of combined opposition from the German princes.

1526 Francis I agrees to the Treaty of Madrid and is released from prison.

1526 The Battle of Mohács takes place. Suleiman the Magnificent defeats Louis, king of Bohemia and Hungary. The king and most of his nobility are killed by the Turks.

1526 Francis I, with the pope, Venice, Florence and the duke of Milan, forms the League of Cognac with the aim of driving the Habsburgs out of Italy.

1527 The duke of Bourbon's German mercenaries sack Rome.

1528 Francis I launches a fresh attack on Italy.

Chronology

1528 While Francis I is away, Louis de Berquin is found guilty of heresy and condemned to be burnt.

1529 The Diet of Speyer meets. Charles V confirms the Edict of Worms against Luther forbidding all ecclesiastical changes. The princes protest in strong terms in the 'Protestation of Disagreement'.

1529 Francis I is defeated at the Battle of Landriano and signs the Peace of Cambrai (The Ladies' Peace) with Charles V.

1530 The Diet of Augsburg is summoned. The Protestants draw up the Confession of Augsburg setting out their Lutheran beliefs. Charles V responds with the *Confutation*. No agreement is reached.

1532 Charles V is present at the defence of Vienna against the Turks.

1532 The Diet of Nuremberg is held. Protestants are promised toleration until a General Council meets.

1532 Francis I orders a second wave of financial reforms.

1533 The theologians, John Calvin and Nicholas Cop, Rector of the university, leave Paris and go into exile (eventually reaching Switzerland).

1533 Francis opens negotiations with the Turkish pirate, Barbarossa.

1534 The Affair of the Placards occurs in France.

1535 The French invade Savoy.

1535 Charles V captures Tunis.

1536 John Calvin's *Institutes of the Christian religion* is published in Basle.

1538 The pope persuades Francis I and Charles V to agree to the Truce of Nice and the two kings come face to face at Aigues-Mortes.

1538–40 Montmorency's influence over Francis I is at its height.

1539 The Ordinance of Villers-Cotterêts, reforming the judicial system, is issued by Francis I.

1539 Charles V appoints his son, Philip, regent of Spain.

1539–40 The citizens of Ghent protest at high taxes and rise up against their regent, Mary of Burgundy. The rebels are crushed by Charles V and his German mercenaries.

1540 Francis I issues the Edict of Fontainebleau giving *Parlements* the right to seek out heretics in France.

1541 The Diet of Regensburg is summoned. Another attempt at constructing a compromise between Lutheran and Roman Catholic beliefs fails.

1541 John Calvin's *Institutes of the Christian religion* is published in French.

1541 Charles V makes an unsuccessful attack on Algiers.

1542 Francis I begins his third wave of financial reforms.

1542–44 Francis I wages war against the Holy Roman Empire and England.

1543 The Turkish pirate, Barbarossa, and his men occupy Toulon.

1544 The Peace of Crépy is signed by Francis I and Charles V.

1545 The Council of Trent opens.

1545 The Treaty of Ardres ends the conflict between Henry VIII and Francis I.

1546 Another Diet is held at Regensburg. Further discussions on a compromise between Roman Catholic and Lutheran beliefs end acrimoniously.

1546 Charles V begins the Schmalkaldic War.

1547 The Protestant princes of the Schmalkaldic League are defeated by Charles V at the Battle of Mühlberg.

1547 Francis I dies.

1547–48 The Diet of Augsburg is held. Charles V issues his *Interim* document, putting forward a compromise between Lutheran and Protestant beliefs. It is strongly resisted by both sides.

1552 Charles V is forced to accept the Convention of Passau by the Protestant princes.

1552 The Treaty of Chambord is signed between Henry II and the League of Protestant princes in Germany.

1555 Charles V abdicates.

1555 The Diet of Augsburg is summoned. The Lutherans are given freedom of worship in the territories where the rulers support them.

1558 Charles V dies at Yuste, in Spain.

1559 The Treaty of Cateau-Cambrésis is signed.

Index